OX.
INDIA SHORT
INTRODUCTIONS

THE INDIAN MIDDLE CLASS

SURINDER S. JODHKA
ASEEM PRAKASH

OXFORD
UNIVERSITY PRESS

OXFORD
UNIVERSITY PRESS

Oxford University Press is a department of the University of Oxford.
It furthers the University's objective of excellence in research, scholarship,
and education by publishing worldwide. Oxford is a registered trademark of
Oxford University Press in the UK and in certain other countries.

Published in India by
Oxford University Press
YMCA Library Building, 1 Jai Singh Road, New Delhi 110 001, India

ISBN-13: 978-0-19-946679-5
ISBN-10: 0-19-946679-3

Typeset in 11/15.6 Bembo Std
by Excellent Laser Typesetters, Pitampura, Delhi 110 034
Printed in India by Replika Press Pvt. Ltd

Contents

Preface

A day after India celebrated the 63rd anniversary of its independence, on the 16th of August 2011, a seventy-four-year-old man named Anna Hazare, a former soldier with the Indian army and a rural farmer from Maharashtra, began an indefinite fast demanding from the Indian government the setting-up of a new institution, the Lokpal, the framework for which was proposed by groups of 'activists' working with him. The proposed institution was expected to oversee the political and bureaucratic class and check corruption in India's public life. Sitting on *dharna* (sit-in protest) and fasting have been popular modes of political protest in India; however, such protests attract the attention of the urban public rarely. This time though it turned out to be different. Not only was his protest reported widely by the press and electronic media, it also generated an unprecedented response and received the active support of the urban public. Though Anna Hazare himself is a *kisan* (a cultivator) and a former *jawan* (a soldier), popular emblems of the India of the 1950s and 1960s, media reports suggested that it is the urban middle class—which acquired strength and visibility during the post-liberalization period, the 1990s and after— that responded to his protest most enthusiastically.

A little more than a year later, on the evening of the 16th of December 2012, a young physiotherapy student was raped and brutally assaulted by six men in a moving bus in Delhi. The woman succumbed to her injuries a few days later. Quite like corruption, rapes and murders are not rare events in cities like Delhi. But this time again, it turned out to be different. The incident was widely reported in popular media and the capital witnessed unprecedented protests in the following days and weeks. Several other cities of India also reported mobilizations of people, protesting against the rape and murder of the young woman in the national capital. Those who participated in these protests came from various cross sections of the urban population but were predominantly from middle-class families.

This growing assertion and ascendance of the Indian middle class became even more pronounced in the following years, especially during the national elections of 2014 and elections for the state assembly in Delhi in 2015. In both these elections, successful campaigns were framed in a language that gave centrality to middle-class aspirations and avoided references to the cleavages of caste and community.

Popular views and analyses of Indian society and its political processes have generally tended to place the differences of caste and community at the centre. Does the emergence of a middle-class identity imply the weakening and probable decline of such ascriptive identities? Many analysts of the contemporary Indian scene would indeed affirm this. They see the ascendance of the middle class as evidence of a fundamental change in social relations and the mental disposition of the common Indian, the *aam aadmi*. This coming of age of the middle class is viewed as the answer to all problems and challenges that India confronts in the 21st century. Once mobilized, they argue, the middle class has the capacity to dislodge the 'corrupt' political

elite and incompetent bureaucracy and turn the country into an efficient and modern nation-state. They
have already proven their worth abroad and can do
so in India, provided that they are allowed to do so by
the 'system'.

However, there are many within the middle class as
well as outside it who view its role with a great deal
of suspicion. The dominant tendency in the Indian
middle class, they argue, has always been to serve its
own interest. The growing influence of the middle
class has tended to produce an exclusionary effect for
those who have historically been on the margins of
Indian society—the Dalits, the Adivasis, and the various
religious minorities. It is this exclusionary tendency of
the upwardly mobile middle-class Indians that keeps
identities of caste and community alive, they would
argue (see Chapter 6). Unlike its counterparts in the
West, the Indian middle class has also been conservative
and tradition-bound, temperamentally.

The emerging scholarly literature on the contemporary dynamics of the Indian middle class also points
to a reconfiguration of the urban family alongside
societal gender relations. Even when the emerging
middle-class cultures make women more visible and

active consumers, it nevertheless reinforces the patriarchal values and traditional practices by not questioning the pre-existing gender divisions in society.

This short book is an attempt to unravel the idea of the Indian middle class, by looking at its origins during the colonial period and the subsequent moments of its expansion during the Nehruvian phase of nation building and after the introduction of economic liberalization during the 1990s. This is not simply a historical account of the middle class as the book also provides a critical overview of the sociology and politics of the Indian middle class, its hegemonic agenda, and its internal diversities. We have tried to write the book in an accessible language while also trying to engage with the subject without sacrificing its complexities and complications.

Acknowledgements

Work on this book began sometime in 2010–11 when the Konrad-Adenauer-Stiftung (KAS), a German Foundation with an office in New Delhi, approached us to write a position paper on the subject for them as a part of their larger project on middle classes in the emerging economies. Working on the Indian middle class was not very difficult. Not only could we find a good volume of written material on the subject, the middle class had also become a buzzword in post-liberalization India.

Besides the in-house discussions with Beatrice Gorawantschy and Susanna Vogt of the KAS Foundation, we were fortunate to receive comments on our rather tentative ideas from a number of academics in India amongst whom our position paper was circulated. This included Dipankar

Gupta, N. Rajaram, Radhika Chopra, Ajay Mehra, and Ashutosh Kumar.

However, this short book took a much longer time to evolve and is very different from what we first wrote for the KAS Foundation. Some of this work was completed when one of us was a visiting faculty at the Lund University in Sweden on a position funded by the Indian Council of Cultural Relations. We would like to acknowledge the positive support from Anna Lindberg, Catarina Kinnval, Staffan Lindberg, Ted Svensson, and Lars Eklund. We are also grateful to Leila Choukroune and Jules Naudet of the Centre for Social Sciences and Humanities (CSSH) in New Delhi for their support. Jules Naudet read the manuscript and offered some very useful and critical comments. Conversations with colleagues at the Centre for the Study of Social Systems (Jawaharlal Nehru University, New Delhi) and the Tata Institute of Social Sciences in Hyderabad helped us in different ways while working on the book. We are particularly grateful to Maitrayee Chaudhuri and Divya Vaid of the Centre for the Study of Social Systems. Comments received from the Oxford University Press reviewers were also very helpful. They helped us revisit some of our formulations and arguments.

Chapters of the book were also read by several of our friends and students. They include Sneha Sudha Komath, Shilpa Deshpande, Priyanka Bawa, Anasua Chatterjee, Suraj Beri, Sreya Sen, and Mallika Chaudhuri. Their comments and suggestions helped us in improving the text and making our language accessible.

While we have tried to write this book as an introductory text, we have tried to bring into our text all the possible complexities of the subject.

Surinder S. Jodhka

Aseem Prakash

Introduction

What does it mean to be middle class in India today? Is it simply an economic category, an income grouping, or something more than that, a group adhering to a certain value system and aspiring to a distinctive style of life? Who would thus qualify to be a middle-class person, and on what criteria? What proportion of the Indian population can be classified as middle class? What role does the middle class play, beyond economics, in culture, in democratic politics, and in shaping India's position in the emerging world order?

Even though the category of middle class has been in use since the days of colonial rule and freedom struggle, it became a buzzword in the everyday life of India only in the early 1990s, after the introduction of economic reforms and neo-liberal policies. Over the years, 'middle class' has come to acquire a kind of generic character. This is perhaps best reflected in its popular translation as the *aam aadmi*, the common person or everyman. Interestingly enough, it is during this period that the notion and popular image of the *aam aadmi* also saw an interesting change, from a tepid, defenceless, and worried person to an aspirational, proud, and acquisitive citizen.

The idea or identity of middle class is invoked in everyday life in contemporary India in a variety of different ways and contexts: urban and educated with a salaried job; qualified and independent professionals; enterprising, mobile, and young women and men; consumers of luxury goods and services; a housewife of an urban family struggling to keep her domestic economy going with a limited income in times of rising prices; an agitated and angry office-goer who always envies his/her neighbour for managing to keep ahead.

Even though being middle class in contemporary India is, in many ways, a matter of privilege, those located in the middle class tend to also view themselves as among those with a fragile sense of security. Along with the poor, they often complain about the manipulative and 'corrupt' economic and political system controlled by the rich and the powerful, the wily elite. Middle-class engagements with politics have been of crucial and critical significance in modern India—from the colonial period to present times. It is the middle class that generally produces leaders who challenge the existing power structures and provide creative directions to social movements of all kinds.

The Indian middle class has also been accused of being a self-serving and self-obsessed category, indifferent to the poor and the marginalized. The middle class creates barriers and boundaries to keep the poor out of its sphere of privileges. On the other end, the poor aspire to join the middle class and work hard to achieve it. Even when they cannot afford to provide wholesome food to their children, they send them to private English medium schools in the hope that education would help them move out of poverty, to middle-class locations.

Besides its invocation in descriptions of social structures and spheres of inequality and power, the idea of the middle class is also invoked, positively, to describe the emerging Indian, who, through education and hard work, is trying to move upwards, with his or her own resources, and, in turn, is transforming the country into a modern and developed nation. It is creative individuals from middle-class India who have been spreading themselves across the most valued and critical avenues of opportunities and expanding the Indian and global economy in neo-liberal times. Globally, mobile computer software engineers and management gurus of Indian origin, who have come to matter almost everywhere in the world today, all come from middle-class families.

The third popular invocation of the middle class is in relation to the market. As an economic agent, the middle-class person is a consumer par excellence. It is the middle class that sustains the modern bourgeois economy through its purchasing power. Given its location, the middle class is presumed to be obsessed with consumption. Consumption for the middle class is not simply an act of economic rationality but also a source of identity. The shopping malls, mobile phones, and growing reach of media are symbolic evidences of the growing significance of the middle class in India. Much of the advertising industry is directed at the middle-class consumer.

Yet, the middle class is not as homogenous as it may appear at the first instance. Diversities within the middle class are many, of income and wealth as also of status and privilege. Middle classes are often sub-classified into the 'upper', the 'lower', and 'those in between' segments, depending upon income, education, occupation, and so on. Similarly, those who call themselves 'middle class' or are classified as such, do not abandon their other identities, particularly those that have been sources of privilege—of caste, community/ religion, and region/ethnicity. Thus, we have notions such as the 'Bengali middle class' or the 'Muslim middle class' or the 'Dalit middle class'. Invariably, the rise and consolidation of such a class within an 'ethnic' or cultural group works to sharpen those identities.

Identifying who belongs to the middle class appears to be quite simple: those in the middle, in between the poor on one end and the rich on the other, are all middle class. Interestingly, this is how most of the contemporary discourse, shaped and shared by economists and policy makers, has been framed. Perhaps the only source of contention for mainstream economists has been the choice of objective criteria, income, consumption, or something else, for drawing the boundaries on the two ends of the middle.

This short book is an attempt to show how such a statistical view is limited and flawed because it tells us very little about the substantive social processes that unfold themselves through the emergence of middle-class social formations and how in turn middle classes in countries like India shape social, cultural, and political life. Middle class for us is a historical and sociological category. It emerges with the development of modern capitalist society, with markets and cities. Its rise implies the emergence of a new kind of social order: a system of ranking and social classification. It transforms the nature of social relations within communities and households, between men and women, and between young and old. While there is something similar about middle classes everywhere in the world, as a historical category, middle classes also have their specificities. Thus, the Indian middle class has its own specific history, sociology, and politics.

We need to understand the dynamics of the Indian middle class because besides being an empirically identifiable sociological category, the middle class has also come to be the norm, that is, the 'normal' way to be, in contemporary India. It has played a kind of hegemonic role since the days of the colonial period, in shaping national identity during the freedom struggle, in shaping the development agenda and nation building after India's independence, and in contemporary times, in creating social consensus on neo-liberal reforms. It is also from within the sections of the middle classes that contests and oppositions to these trends in Indian society are articulated. Thus, besides being a short introduction to the Indian middle class, this book, we hope, will also open a window to an understanding of contemporary Indian society, its pasts, and its possible futures.

1

What Does It Mean to Be Middle Class?

> The emergence of a middle class marks a decisive moment in a nation's history. It indicates an open rather than a closed opportunity structure, a society with the chance of upward mobility and achievement beyond subsistence. It further marks the transition from an industrial society, polarized into the antagonistic classes of propertied and property-less, to one with buffering groups in the middle.... (Landry and Marsh 2011: 374)

India has often been described as a land of contradictions. The discourse of the Indian middle class is a good example of this. A few simple facts make it evident. In terms of real income or purchasing power parity,

India today is the third largest economy of the world. Only the United States of America and China are larger than India in terms of the absolute size of its economic activity. India is also home to a large number of the rich and wealthy. The absolute size of those who could be described as rich and middle class in India today is larger than the total population of the relatively big countries of Europe: Germany, France, and Britain.

However, the other side of the reality in India is equally, if not more, compelling and important. Even in the second decade of the 21st century, India is home to the largest number of the chronically poor in the world, larger than Sub-Saharan Africa, and nearly one-third of all the desperately poor in the world. Together, they also account for nearly one-third of India's total population. The poor in India lack the basic facilities for a secure and dignified human life. As per most indicators of economic and human development, India continues to be a developing country. Despite its comparatively high rates of growth, India still does not figure among the top 100 countries in the United Nations Development Programme (UNDP) ranking based on comparative human development.

Social life in India, too, is marked by some very interesting contrasts and contradictions. As per the Census of 2011, a little more than two-thirds of the Indian population lives in over half a million of its rural settlements. In states like Bihar and Himachal Pradesh, their numbers go up to nearly 90 per cent. A good proportion of those living in rural India depend directly on agriculture for their livelihood. Agriculture was reported to be the primary source of employment for more than half of all working Indians. However, the share of agriculture in India's national gross domestic product (GDP) has been consistently declining, and had come down to less than one-seventh of the total income by early 2015.

As would be the case with agrarian settlements in other parts of the world, ownership and non-ownership of land carries a lot of value in social, economic, and cultural life in rural India. However, traditionally rural settlements in most of India (though not everywhere) have also been divided along caste lines, in a hierarchical structure, governed by values of purity and impurity where the normative order divided village residents into communities and ranked them vertically. Even when the hierarchical order of caste overlapped with patterns of landownership, its logic was different. It was based on notions of status, honour, and humiliation. It also marked rigid boundaries across communities and restricted social interaction and marriage alliances across caste groups.

There is no space for a 'middle class' in such an imagination. Those located in the middle of the caste hierarchy, or in the land ownership pattern, do not qualify to be middle class. The systemic logic of caste does not allow for individual mobility. Similarly, the 'middle peasants' of agrarian societies are not middle classes, because of their attachment to land and their dependence on subsistence agriculture.

Middle class, as it has come to be viewed in contemporary times, is a category of modern society, a society that emerged with industrial development and urbanization in the modern West. Middle class is not a community with an ascriptive identity. It emerged in the Indian subcontinent only with the introduction of a Western-style secular education system, the industrial economy, and a new administrative system by the British colonial rulers during the 19th century. Over the years, the Indian middle class has continued to grow.

After India's independence from colonial rule, the new developmental state expanded its bureaucratic structure manifold and invested large sums of money in public sector enterprises. It also built more schools, universities, and hospitals. Private capital also grew, albeit slowly. As a consequence of these processes of economic development, the size of the Indian middle class steadily grew. Beginning with the 1990s, the Indian middle class began to acquire much greater visibility. Economic reforms introduced by the Indian political regime significantly enhanced its engagements with the global economy. The onset of a new process of globalization also enabled India to participate actively in emergent areas of what was being described as the 'new economy'. By incentivizing private capital and encouraging investments by foreign capital, the 'neo-liberal' economic reforms also raised growth rates of the Indian economy quite significantly. From a sluggish pace of around 3 per cent during the first four decades after independence, the Indian economy began to grow at 7 to 8 per cent per annum, and occasionally at even higher rates.

A distinctive feature of this rapid economic growth has been its urban-centric nature. The size of India's urban economy, particularly its service sector, has been growing quite steadily. Even though the process of economic liberalization has benefited private capital, the expanding service economy has increased the size of the middle classes rapidly and substantially. The middle class also grew within the expanding private manufacturing economy. With growing numbers, the influence of the middle classes in Indian society and its political system also grew. Besides a manifold increase in its size, India's new middle class has also been getting richer and internally more diverse.

At another level, these processes of economic growth and expanding middle classes are fundamentally transforming the structure of the Indian society and its economy, from being characterized by 'a sharp contrast between a small elite and a large impoverished mass, to being one with substantial intermediate classes' (Sridharan 2008:1). Some scholars have also argued that this change provides the necessary economic and political base to the emerging market-based capitalist economy in the rapidly changing world today (Kohli 1989).

While no one would disagree with the fact that the size of the middle classes in India has indeed increased quite substantially since the beginning of the economic reforms in the early 1990s, there are several disagreements on the exact numbers of those who could be described as the middle classes, and their proportions in the total population of India. These estimates vary significantly and range from a lower end of 5 or 6 per cent of the total population of the country to an upper end of 25 or 30 per cent, and, sometimes, even more. However, almost everyone agrees that the size of the Indian middle class will continue to grow, at least for several decades to come. This is in contrast to many countries of the Western hemisphere and some other parts of the developed world, such as Japan, where the middle classes have reportedly been shrinking. Thanks largely to the growing numbers of middle-class consumers, India is being viewed as one of those countries where the markets will keep expanding for quite some time to come. Despite its enormous social and economic problems, India is listed amongst the most happening places in the world today, an emerging global economic power (see Chapter 5).

The rise of the Indian middle class is also transforming the popular image of India as well as that of Indians.

The old orientalist representation of India as a land of snake charmers, village communities, and spiritual gurus is slowly giving way to a new picture. India's weight in the global economy continues to increase because of its technically and culturally skilled human power, which is willing to travel across continents and adapt to a variety of working conditions. The middle class is also beginning to lobby in the internal politics of the country for reshaping its political institutions and its systems of governance.

The Classical Conceptions

The 'middle class' has been an elusive and yet popular category. While recent writings by Indian economists have mostly debated its size in terms of incomes and consumption levels, the term has a broader sociological and conceptual history, both in the Western context as well as in India. As a modern sociological category, it emerged in Western Europe with the rise of industrial capitalism during the 18th and 19th centuries, and continued to expand conceptually and empirically during the 20th century. Karl Marx was perhaps the first social scientist who provided a comprehensive analysis of an emerging industrial society through his concepts of capitalism and class.

Even though he used the category of class while discussing pre-capitalist societies as well, the term 'middle class' is invoked primarily in the analysis of capitalist societies. For Marx, capitalism, or the bourgeois society, was a class society structured around the relationship between two fundamental classes, the bourgeoisie and the proletarian. The bourgeoisie, the owners of the means of production or the capital, exploited the proletariat or the working classes, who in order to survive had to sell their labour power to the owners of capital.

While the two fundamental classes were tied to each other through an exploitative system, there were some who had not yet been subsumed by the capitalist system. They were neither wageworkers employed by anyone nor did they hire others. They were shopkeepers, small peasants, independent professionals, artisans, and other such people. In social science literature, these groups have come to be known as the 'old middle classes', a residual category.

Marx did not think that they would survive as independent economic actors for very long and the logic of capitalist development would eventually swallow them up, subsuming them in one of the two major classes. While some sections of these old middle classes indeed declined with the development of capitalist economies, some continued to survive and flourish within the capitalist production system. More importantly, newer categories of professionals—such as doctors, teachers, bankers, public administrators, architects, engineers, and managers—who either worked independently or were employed in supervisory services and earned decent salaries, swelled over time. Even though, technically speaking, the owners of capital employed them on a salary, they did not see themselves as members of the 'working classes', nor did they support the proletarian class concerns.

Marx had called them 'ideological classes', who produced 'false-consciousness' and the hegemonic cultural edifice for the ruling bourgeois regime. Later, Marxists also studied these 'new middle-classes' and tried to conceptualize them in a variety of different ways. While some looked at them as bearers of cultural capital (Gouldner 1979) and new petty-bourgeoisie (Poulantzas 1975), others viewed them as occupying 'contradictory class locations', being beneficiaries of the capitalist mode of production and simultaneously being a part of the proletariat as they too had to sell their intellectual labour for a wage (Wright 1978: 61–3). The contemporary Marxist scholarship recognizes the fact that the middle classes have not only survived the growth of capitalism but have also expanded in size over the years (Wright 1979: 64–82).

Perhaps the most important contribution of the Marxist notion of class is its emphasis on it being a social or relational category and not simply an income-based or economic classification. It is only through their relationship to others that a category could be identified as being distinct.

Another German sociologist, Max Weber (1946), too wrote extensively on class. Though he initially claimed to be only 'reformulating' Marx's ideas, he eventually ended up offering a different conception of class and the middle classes. For Weber, class, as a category of distinction, acquires significance in capitalism and the market-driven economy, in which individuals compete for economic gains. He defines classes as groups of people who share a similar 'market situation'.

Weber also works with a pluralistic and differentiated conception of classes. He begins by making a distinction between the propertied, the 'ownership classes' (*Besitzklassen*) and the property-less, the 'acquisition classes' (*Erwerbsklassen*). However, unlike Marx, Weber does not see them as two 'basic class' positions. They are internally differentiated. For example, while the 'rentiers' and the 'entrepreneurs' are both 'owners of capital', sociologically they are two very different categories. Similarly the 'property-less' are also differentiated in relation to 'types and degree of monopolization' of the marketable skills which they possess:

> Consequently, there are various types of middle classes, which stand between the positively privileged classes (the propertied) and the negatively privileged classes (those who possess neither property nor marketable skills). While these groupings are all nominally property-less, those who possess skills, which have definite 'market value', are certainly in different class situation from those who have nothing to offer but their (unskilled) labour. In acquisition classes—i.e., those associated particularly with the rise of modern capitalism—educational qualifications take on a particular significance in this respect.... (Giddens 1981: 43)

Another important feature of Weber's analysis is his distinction between 'class' and 'status-groups'. Unlike class, where 'economic interest in market relationship' is the defining feature, status groups are 'communities' as they are 'built upon criteria of grouping other than those stemming from market situations'. Status groups are defined by their specific 'styles of life'. Interestingly, for Weber, consumption is an aspect of one's 'style of life' and not 'class situation'. Class situation stems primarily from one's relationship with the process of production (presumably goods and services). In other words, consumption patterns produce 'status groups' and not 'classes'. Further, unlike Marx, Weber does not see any tendency towards polarization of society into two classes. On the contrary, Weber argues that with the development of capitalism, the white collar 'middle class' would tend to expand rather than disappear.

While Marx and Weber differ in their understanding of middle classes, they also tend to agree on several basic points. Both treat 'middle class' as a modern category, which emerges with the development of industrial capitalism and the market economy. They also agree that class is an economic category, a material relationship, and not a 'mental disposition'. Though, at

13

an analytical level, Marx proposes a two-class model, he too recognizes the plural character of the middle class. For example, his notion of 'ideological classes' is not very different from Weber's notion of 'educated middle-classes'.

Another sociologist, Pierre Bourdieu, has made an important addition to our understanding of the social dynamics of class. Instead of focussing purely on economic relations or market situation of individuals, he underlines the need to look at the variety of resources individuals have: social networks, education, and other cultural habits, besides the economic resources. They too work 'as actually usable resources and powers' for those who possess them (Bourdieu 1984: 114). For example, social networks and the quality of education play crucial roles in the economic possibilities or opportunities a person would have in the present day society. This indeed helps in empirical study of the middle class and its reproduction in everyday life.

Further, Bourdieu also disagrees with Marx and Weber on the question of theoretically specifying boundaries between different classes; instead, he underlines the need to focus on the practice. However, the social context, or habitus, the socially constituted systems of dispositions that orient 'thoughts, perceptions, expressions, and actions' (Bourdieu 1990: 55), is also central to his analysis of human action. Thus, social classes do not have a pre-assigned political position and the boundaries, for example, between working class and the middle class are not as neatly marked as often presumed in the theoretical discussion of scholars like Marx and Weber.

It is in this broad framework of understanding of middle classes that we will later try to discuss the Indian case.

Middle Class in the West

Sociologists and historians of modern Western societies have also studied different dimensions of the middle classes in these societies. Many of them have worked with the Marxist distinction between the 'old' and the 'new' middle classes.

The well-known economic historian Karl Polanyi has extensively explored the emergence of class-based divisions in Europe and the distinctiveness of social relations that emerged with the development of modern day market-based economies. He, too, locates their origin in the great social transformations that occurred with commercial and industrial revolutions in the West and the subsequent rise of the capitalist economic system. Following the European sociological tradition, Polanyi described the change in social relationships that the industrial revolution produced as a movement from 'customs' to 'contract' (Polanyi 1957). Perhaps the most significant change in this context was the emergence of the market as an institution for ordering economic transactions. This also meant that things like land and labour could be bought and sold in the markets through money at a price, determined at the intersection of demand and supply. How did this shift produce a class society?

As we have mentioned in the context of the caste system in India, Polanyi too argues that the economic and social relations in pre-modern Europe followed a different logic. Quite like the caste system in India, social status, derived from a traditional normative system, determined economic rewards. In custom-driven societies, movement of goods and services was subjected to the rigid rights and obligations of the status-based normative order (age, sex, kinship, marriage). The rise of the market society transformed the nature

16

of exchange relationships. They had to be based on the logic of supply and demand, which operated through contracting. A contract is intrinsically individualistic. It mandates economic transaction to the free will of the individual, which manifests in a legal agreement. Individuals are no longer identified by their status in the hierarchical system of social order, but instead are identified through the kind of services they could offer in the market place.

This shift towards a market society operating through contract gave birth to a distinct social pyramid. On the top of the social pyramid were the gentry and aristocracy. These were usually men of independent means, but not necessarily landowners, who had their own private income and did not have to work for a living. Mostly they lived idly and without manual labour. At the lowest end of the social pyramid were the labouring poor, the working class, who were hired through the markets and who dirtied their hands. Between these extremes were the middling people, who worked but did not get their hands dirty. The majority of them were commercial or industrialist capitalists who had control over money drawn through parental gift, inheritance, or loan, which they invested to earn more money. Along with the upper class, they also employed the working class who had no stock of money and were dependent on others for their living (Earle 1989: 3).

The emergent classes in the upper segment of the social pyramid, thus, employed the working class and invested capital to enable it to accumulate on a regular basis. Earle does not think that men of letters—clergy, lawyers, physicians—belonged to the upper or middle classes. Unlike the upper class they were not idle, nor did they use capital to earn profit like the middle class. This educated class relied mainly on salaries and fees. These professionals, argues Earle, occupied an intermediate position between the upper and middle classes. Further, some of them, such as the bishops as well as most barristers and physicians, were clearly members of the upper class. However, towards the 17th century, the younger generation of upper-class families started pursuing trade or went into the service of the church, while the daughters married merchants (Earle 1989: 3–10).

Academic accounts analysing socio-economic relationships differ on the extent to which the economy was 'dis-embedded' from customs (Gemici 2007), and also on the extent to which the emergent modern economy could generate a middle class across different regions of Europe (Wahrman 1995). Yet the shift towards contract was sufficiently large to enable a substantial proportion of people (merchants, bankers, traders, and so on) to reach the middle rung of the social pyramid. Gradually, the middle class grew in numbers and social power. The new social reality was eventually reflected in England through the Reform Bill of 1832 that allowed the admission of the middle class into the parliament, which hitherto had been the preserve of the landed elite. As in England and other parts of Europe, the idea of the middle class as a social group was further cemented with the political representation of this class in both political and public spheres (Wahrman 1995). Gradually, the middle class was recognized as a class not only of economic power but also of specific social manners, morals, and values, which were considered integral to its formation and growth (French 1996; Owensby 1999). From a section of this middle class eventually emerged the rich ruling class of capitalist society, the bourgeoisie, and as discussed by Marx and others, the term 'middle classes' began to be used for those who remained outside the new order of wage labour and capital.

Most sociologists attribute the emergence of the 'new middle class' to the further expansion of industrial capitalism and the rise of big corporations with large and complex organizational structures. G.D.H. Cole (1950), a well-known sociologist, attributes the birth of the new middle class to two important developments in the Western economy: first, an increase in the number of public schools and the spread of education; and second, the spread of joint-stock companies. These developments fostered large-scale enterprise and brought into existence a new class of salaried managers and administrators. Lockwood, another sociologist, also attributes the rise of the white-collared salaried class to the developments of corporate capitalism and the emergence of big organizations (Lockwood 1958).

The crucial difference between the 'old' and the 'new' middle classes is their position within the economy. The old middle classes occupied that position by the virtue of their being placed outside the polar class structure. They were neither part of the capitalist class nor of the working class. The new middle classes, on the other hand, did not enjoy any such autonomy. They were part of the big organizations. Their intermediate position came from their place inside the industrial economy. Their growth occurred because of the new demands of modern industry that required the services of a large number of specialists and professionals with technical and administrative skills.

The 'new' middle classes further expanded with growth of the 'tertiary' or the service sector of the economy (Dahrendorf 1959). Along with urbanization and industrialization, a large number of tertiary industries, such as banking, insurance, hospitals, hotels, tourism, and the mass media developed. The proportion of this segment has been consistently growing in the working population in most of the industrialized countries of the West.

The discourse of the middle class experienced another interesting shift in the West during the first half of the 20th century when the middle class became a more generalized category and a social identity. The rise of the welfare state and strong trade unions produced a new category of *the affluent worker* (Goldthrope 1963), whose wages allowed him or her to access middle-class lifestyles. The democratic welfare state expanded the domain of citizenship rights and began to universally provide quality education, medical care, and basic housing for free (Marshall 1950). The welfare state system also had to take care of all the basic requirements of those who were on the margins, such as the aged, the disabled, and the unemployed.

Developed countries of western Europe, North America, and the Pacific thus virtually became 'middle-class societies'. Not that these countries had no economic disparities, but a large majority of their populations, going up to 75 to 90 per cent, identified themselves as being members of different segments of the middle class.[1] Middle class thus came to be identified as 'everyman', which could be translated in the present day Indian context as *aam aadmi*.[2]

The erstwhile developed countries have been through a rather severe economic crisis since the early years of the 21st century. The gradual weakening of the welfare state and a prolonged economic crisis have

[1] http://www.gallup.com/poll/159029/americans-likely-say-belong-middle-class.aspx.

[2] Interestingly, the category *aam aadmi*, as it has come to be understood in the Indian urban context, is not only gendered, referring to *aadmi* (man) to the exclusion of *aurat* (woman), but is also a category that refers primarily to urban middle and lower middle classes, excluding the poor—urban as well as rural.

had a direct impact, particularly on the income levels of the lower segments of their middle classes, and consequently for their self-image as middle classes. The shrinkage of the middle class in most of the developed world is not merely a matter of perception.

The idea and the rise of the *aam aadmi* as the middle class in India has a different trajectory, which we explore in the following chapters of this book.

2

The Formative Years

> The colonial middle class ... was simultaneously
> placed in a position of subordination in one relation
> and in a position of dominance in another.... For
> the ... middle class of the late nineteenth century,
> political and economic domination by a British colo-
> nial elite was a fact. The class was created in a relation
> of subordination. But its contestation of this relation
> was to be premised upon its cultural leadership of the
> indigenous colonized people. The nationalist project
> was in principle a hegemonic project. (Chatterjee
> 1993: 36)

Societies and ideas do not 'evolve' through a simple
process of diffusion, as a linear progression. Even
though, over the past century and more, the market-
based capitalist economic system has spread across

different regions of the world, local histories of its spread and development have been very different from what happened in the West during the 19th and 20th centuries. Past realities and local histories of different regions and their cultures actively shape outcomes of economic processes. Even when technological or political revolutions reorder social relations, new social categories carry the stamps of their pasts. For example, the history of industrialization and capitalist development and the new social orders in countries like China, Brazil, South Africa, Russia, or even Japan have been different from what is considered as the 'classical' Western model spelt out in textbooks of economic history and classical sociology. This is true about the middle classes as well, including the Indian middle class.

Despite their obvious suggestion, the recent processes of globalization and increasing economic integration have not been able to erase diversities and differences across regions and nations of the world. Globalization does not mean social homogenization. Diversities and differences persist, not only in the innocuous spheres of culture and habit, such as food, dialect, or rituals, but also in larger structures, such as the modes of political organization, social institutions, and even in market-based processes. Even newly emergent economic spheres such as corporate businesses tend to exhibit distinctive sociological characters, derived from their past histories and their local/regional contexts. India's contemporary history is a case in point.

Perhaps the single most important fact about contemporary Indian society is its history of colonization by the British. India, as we know it today, obtained its form and administrative systems largely during the colonial period. Its present day geographic boundaries and identity of a nation-state were also shaped and acquired at the time of Independence and Partition in 1947.

The Indian middle class also evolved during this period, out of the new educational system introduced by the British during the early decades of the 19th century to produce a class of local *babu*s (literally, clerks), who would help the colonial rulers rule over the expanding territories of the empire. The oft-quoted extract from Thomas. B. Macaulay's *Minutes*, dated the 2 February 1835, sums up this formative intent of the colonial rulers quite clearly. As a member of the colonial bureaucracy in India, Macaulay had argued with his colleagues about the need for initiating a new education system in India:

> … to form a class who may be interpreters between us and the millions whom we govern, a class of persons Indian in blood and colour, but English in tastes, in opinions, in morals and in intellect. To that class we may leave it to refine the vernacular dialects of the country, to enrich those dialects with terms of science borrowed from the Western nomenclature, and to render them by degrees fit vehicles for conveying knowledge to the great mass of the population.[1]

As is evident from this and other historical accounts, the intention of the British rulers was not to produce a middle class that would creatively innovate and participate in the economic process of the emerging bourgeois economic order of the region, but to train a dependent category that would facilitate the British not only in their needs for administration but also in generating a cultural hegemony. This class was to be

[1] 'Macaulay's Minute on Education, February 2, 1835', available at http://home.iitk.ac.in/~hcverma/Article/Macaulay-Minutes.pdf (accessed on 8 August 2014).

an agency to enable the natives to learn about the per-ceived superior knowledge systems prevalent in Great Britain and the other virtues of Western civilization.

As the popular view goes, the new class of *babu*s evolved into an agency that effectively mediated between the colonial rulers and local masses and became the most important vehicle to spread the 'superior' Western culture, its message of modernity, including the ideas of democracy, which also produced conflict between the local *babu* and the colonial boss, eventually taking the shape of the freedom movement. According to this common sense, the Western-educated middle class of India continues to be a modernizing social category, an important agent of positive social change in Indian society, where the hold of tradition continues to be a critical source of its backwardness.

While the colonial context of its origin is indeed a fact, this celebratory representation of the Indian middle class is a myth that, to a large extent, is pro-duced by members of the Indian middle classes themselves. It helps them perpetuate their position of privilege and power. The actual history of the Indian middle class is far more complex, diverse, and simply different.

The Indian middle class did not just emerge as a modernizing agent out of its traditional moorings. It did not evolve as a distinct social group/category detached from its past history and existing social contexts. On the contrary, in certain cases, the middle class championed 'tradition', and actively represented and constructed local level 'sectarian' identities. A good example of this is the manner in which they were able to reproduce patriarchal authority and a notion of Indian family that reproduced the position of women as homemakers through actively eulogizing their roles as mothers and the guardians of native traditions. Similarly, the colonial policies of classifying communities on clearly marked caste and religious identities sharpened ascriptive boundaries among groups and communities. The British did not always wish to change the pre-existing social realities. On the contrary, they actively participated in the production of a new common sense about India. They often absorbed the 'traditional' view into their policy frames and reinforced, and at times even strengthened, the pre-existing structures of social relations. In other words, they simultaneously transformed and reinforced the pre-existing structures of power relations. The

Indian middle classes were at the centre of all these processes.

Colonial Rule and Social Change

Despite continuities and compromises, the British colonial rule over the subcontinent turned out to be fundamentally different from all the earlier political systems and empires that had existed in the region. The British not only established their rule over a much larger territory of the region compared to any prior ruler in the history of the region, they also transformed the diverse economies and political cultures of the subcontinent. Their agrarian policies had far-reaching implications for the existing structure of land relations and the manners in which cultivators and landowners engaged with the state and with each other.

The new Land Settlements transformed patterns of revenue collections from the cultivators. They also initiated the process of commercialization of agricultural production, without modernizing it; integrating the local cultivators into market economy without enabling them to bargain and compete. As a consequence, India's agrarian economy declined.

Pre-colonial India also had an urban economy and vibrant artisanal industries, which suffered and declined when the British imported cheap goods from the factories in Britain where the industrial revolution had transformed their technological base and productive capacity. This 'de-industrialization' of the erstwhile urban economy of India added to the burden on agricultural lands.

On the positive side, they introduced railways and modern industries in the subcontinent. They reorganized the political and administrative structures of the colonial empire and introduced modern modes of communication. The task of administering an expanding empire needed an increasing number of skilled human resources.

The British initiated a process of educating the 'natives' by opening schools and colleges in different parts of the subcontinent. These educational institutions first appeared in the new colonial cities like Calcutta, Bombay, and Madras (now known as Kolkata, Mumbai, and Chennai respectively). Local communities, particularly those with resources and high social standing, responded enthusiastically and sent their children for 'modern' education. Historians of modern

India claim that by the 1880s, the number of English-educated Indians was already around 50,000 (Sarkar 1983: 65) and increased quite rapidly soon after. The number of those studying in these English medium schools rose from 298,000 to 505,000 in just around 20 years, from 1887 to 1907 (Sarkar 1983: 65).

English was not to be merely a language of the school. It soon began to acquire the stature of a superior medium of communication among the embryonic middle-class elite. This is clearly indicated by the fact that the circulation of English language newspapers rose quite rapidly during this period, from around 90,000 in 1885 to nearly 276,000 in 1905 (Sarkar 1983: 65).

B.B. Mishra, who was among the first Indian scholars to write a detailed book on *The Indian Middle Class*, published by the Oxford University Press in 1961, tells us that by 1911, British India had established as many as 186 colleges in different parts of the empire, teaching 36,284 students. These numbers went up to 231 colleges and 59,595 students by 1921 and to 385 colleges and 144,904 students by 1939 (Mishra 1961: 304). Manifestly, there was an enthusiasm for Western education, particularly for higher education in English.

Seeing this enthusiasm, the British government began to reduce its grants for the purpose. This encouraged private players and trusts to open schools and colleges, which helped in continued expansion of educational infrastructure. According to one estimate, the number of private colleges increased from 11 to 53 between 1881–2 and 1901–2 (Sarkar 1983: 67). Some rich Indian families even sent their children abroad, mostly to England, for further education in leading British universities, such as Oxford, Cambridge, and London. After securing degrees from these prestigious institutions, many returned home. This new native elite also brought with them modern ideas of 'liberalism' and 'democracy' that had become popular in the West after the French Revolution. Thus, they became carriers of not only British cultural values but also of modern ideas of freedom, equality, and democracy.

Those educated in local colleges were mostly absorbed in the colonial administrative structure. These jobs in the colonial government carried a 'high' social status and became a route to acquiring middle-class positions. Over the years, a new class emerged in India. Apart from those employed in the administrative jobs of the British government, they included independent professionals such as lawyers, doctors, teachers, medics, and journalists. The size of this 'educated middle class' thus continued to grow during the second half of the 19th century.

Economic Changes and the Expansion of 'Other' Middle Classes

Apart from the newly introduced sphere of English-medium education, economic changes introduced by the colonial government also expanded several other spheres of the Indian economy, which produced newer social groups and enlarged the size of older groups, who could be described as middle classes. The most prominent among them were the petty traders/shop-keepers and independent artisans, the social groups that were called 'old middle classes' in the Western context. Merchants and artisans had always been separate social strata at the local level in economic structures of most regions of the subcontinent. They could easily be identified through their separate caste identities.

They were an organic part of local communities. As the economy began to change in response to the new administrative policies of the colonial rulers, many of the merchants moved to newly emerging towns and cities and became independent traders. This process was further accelerated during the post-Independence period.

Though limited in its significance, modern machine-based industry also began to grow during the colonial period. The establishment of the railways during the middle of the 19th century created conditions for the growth of modern industry in India. The colonial rulers had laid railways in the subcontinent primarily for transporting raw materials from the region required for the British industry overseas. However, once the railways were established, the British also invested in local industry in not only big cities but also in far-flung areas, such as plantations in the Northeast.

The growing economic activity gave boost to trade and mercantile activity and some of the local traders accumulated enough savings to be able to invest in modern industry. The *swadeshi* movement started by the nationalist leadership during the early decades of 20th century gave a further boost to native industry. Apart from giving employment to the labour force, this industry also employed white-collared skilled workers. Thus, along with those employed in administrative positions by the colonial rulers, the growing numbers of these white-collared employees of the new industrial sector also added to the size of the middle classes during the colonial period.

Social Origins and Status Hierarchies

In his historical survey of the colonial period, historian Sumit Sarkar demonstrates how the English-educated Bengali middle class (lawyers, teachers, medics, journalists) 'diligently cultivated the self-image', which represented them as a superior class, above the lay toilers of land, though below the traditionally dominant Bengali upper-caste *zamindar*s (Sarkar 1983: 67). However, unlike their Western counterparts, the social origins of this class did not lie in industry and trade, which remained under control of the British companies or local trading communities, such as the Marwaris, and other such castes/communities. While most of the educated modern professionals came from relatively privileged social backgrounds and had some connections with land, they generally occupied intermediary positions in the prevailing tenurial structure. In terms of their position in the traditional ritual hierarchies, almost all of them came from relatively upper segments of the caste system.

A similar pattern could be observed in Madras and Pune where Western-educated groups had strong connections with petty landholdings and petty rent collecting communities (Sarkar 1983: 68–9). Bombay saw the emergence of a proto kind of alliance between the mill-owners and a group called the Bombay Intelligentsia on issues like abolition of import duties on Lancashire cotton and the imposition of counter-vailing excise (Sarkar 1983: 68). These origins of the middle classes from the landed and propertied, as we discuss later in another chapter of this book, shaped their politics in relation to the developmental process during the post-Independence period. Their own linkages with landed interests structured their attitudes towards policies for agrarian change, such as the Land Reforms, initiated by the government of independent India after 1947.

Middle Class as Social Reformers

Western education was not simply a process of learn-ing skills or mastering a foreign language. It exposed individuals to a different culture, a different religion, and a different set of values. While they would have been proud servants of the Raj, their growing proximity to the British White-Christian culture also made them reflect on their own culture. Given that a large majority of them came from the upper segment of traditional hierarchies and relatively secure social backgrounds, they did not wish to simply abandon their moorings. While many aspects of Western culture influenced them, they did not want to be swept away by it. They were enchanted by Western modernity, but they also felt threatened by it. They were particularly worried about the possible expansion of Christianity, along with the spread of Western values. They chose to critically examine their culture and initiate reforms, often in collaboration with the colonial masters, so that they could strengthen their own 'traditions'.

In some regions of the subcontinent, these newly educated individuals initiated a variety of social reform movements during the 19th and early 20th centuries. These reform movements were most pronounced among the upper caste Hindus, but they were not confined to them. Muslims, Sikhs, and those from lower orders of the caste hierarchy also initiated reforms within their own contexts. Even though the reforms touched different segments of their communities, members of the middle class almost everywhere provided the leadership to these initiatives.

The middle-class leaders of these movements worked for a negotiated adaptation of Western modernity. They underlined the need for retaining what they saw as the core of the traditional religious belief and culture, and simultaneously learning from Western and Christian cultures. Even though they had their regional character, these movements emerged almost in all regions of India: in Bengal in the east, in Madras in the south, in Bombay and Pune in the West, and in Punjab in the north. The two most important reform movements of these among the Hindus were the Brahmo Samaj, initiated in 1828, and the Arya Samaj, initiated in 1875. Both these movements were led by Western-educated upper caste and middle-class Hindus, Ram Mohan Roy and Swami Dayanand respectively, and they both explicitly stated their agenda as saving Hinduism from the threat of Christianity through internal reforms, to re-tune it, and to adapt it to modernity.

In case of such reforms among the Hindus, the narrative was to selectively reinvent the past tradition and glorify it in order to claim its superiority over Western Christianity. This re-invention and glorification of the ancient past also implied acceptance and advocacy of 'tradition', albeit in a reformed format, which included the hierarchical social order of *varna* and caste, presided over by the Brahmins. Unlike in the West, where middle classes were part of the processes of secularization and individualization, members of the Indian middle classes invested their own identities in communities and their perceived traditions that they reinvented through these reform movements. Their quest for the so-called social reforms eventually produced 'new', and sometimes more rigid, cultural boundaries across and within the pre-existing communities.

Even when some of these reformers publicly rejected practices such as superstitions, devotional belief, or the practice of Sati, they used religious symbolism for political mobilizations and public/intellectual debates. A historian of colonial India, Lata Mani, shows how middle-class reformers underlined the greatness of the Sanskritic Hindu tradition even when they collaborated with the British rulers on the legislation banning Sati:

> The debate on *sati* was shaped by a specifically colonial discourse, which simultaneously privileged brahmanic scriptures as the locus of authentic tradition and constituted woman as a site for the contestation of tradition. (Mani 1999: 2)

Thus, the debates on Sati during the colonial period produced a notion of Indian tradition which has had far-reaching implications for the shaping of the so-called Indian and native views of gender and caste, as also of nation and citizenship. The discourse on Sati privileged the Brahmin interpretation of select Hindu texts as the only source of an authentic understanding of tradition, ignoring the actual custom and practice. Similarly, as Mani argues, 'women and brahmanic scriptures became interlocking grounds for this re-articulation. Women became emblematic of tradition, and the reworking of traditions was conducted largely through debating their rights and status in society' (Mani 1987: 121–2).

Middle-class activists also tried to rhetorically present a singular imagined Hindu community, even though the notion of a single Hindu community did not go well with the hierarchical social order. The politics of the Indian middle class during the colonial period remained caught in contradictions and tensions between the 'old and new', the 'hierarchical and emancipatory', and 'religious and secular', eventually producing a 'fractured modernity', to use Sanjay Joshi's term (Joshi 2001).

Quest for Power and Imaginings of India

The growing enthusiasm of this newly emergent English–educated middle class for social reforms clearly reflected their growing aspiration to project themselves to the colonial masters as leaders of the local/native communities. Their proximity to the colonial masters and their willingness to speak to their own communities on behalf of the British rulers gave them a new role, that of mediators. Not only did they demonstrate the virtues of Western civilization to the natives but also emerged as natural representatives of the natives.

This was also aided by the British view of Indian society. They did not see the Indians as being constituted through associations of individuals. For them, the

Indians were made of communities, of caste, religion, and kinship. These were not simple notional issues of perception. They deployed these notions in their systems of governance. They, for example, 'encouraged the members of each community to present their case in communitarian terms' (Grewal 1989: 195). This had serious implications. Communities were to become fundamental to perceived nature of Indian society. In collaboration with the emergent middle-class elite, colonial policies often worked towards sharpening of communitarian boundaries, across and within religious and linguistic communities.

In his historical work on Lucknow and northern India, Sanjay Joshi (2001) rightly shows how, through their cultural activism, the newly educated members of the middle classes established their cultural authority. After being educated in colonial institutions, members of the middle class initiated a new kind of civic activism in the public sphere. They started publishing newspapers, magazines, and literary journals. They formed civic associations. Members of the newly emergent middle class did not do it to serve universal interests but to establish their own position as the new leaders of a changing India. This politics of the middle class was so constructed in the public sphere that their socio-cultural and political agenda was distinct from the existing traditional feudal elite. However, they did not wish to dislodge the feudal elite through a democratic discourse of citizenship. On the contrary, they simultaneously invoked traditional prejudices to exclude lower castes and classes from participation in the public sphere. This 'led them to establish the difference from [other social groups] and assert power over the British rulers. Through such projects a distinctive middle-class identity emerged' (Joshi 2001: 8).

Thus the middle class in colonial northern India came to acquire a prestige and a position of leadership less through their economic standing in the traditional social order, and more through, what Joshi describes as, their effective 'cultural entrepreneurship' in the public sphere. In Lucknow,

> the people who came to be termed middle-class in colonial India... belonged to the upper strata of society, without being at the very top. Most of them were upper-caste Hindus or Ashraf (high born) Muslims, and many came from so called service communities, that is families and social groups who had traditionally

served in the courts of indigenous rulers and large landlords. Not only did this mean that such men had enough economic resources but also they possessed sufficient educational training to shape and participate in public debates during the colonial era.... Merely the knowledge of English, similarity of family background and even the exposure to western education did not transform Ashrafs, Kyasthas, Brahmins, Khatris or Baniyas of north India into a middle class. This was achieved through cultural entrepreneurship. (Joshi 2001: 7)

As the middle class expanded in size, its political aspirations also grew. They aspired for more share in the state power. It is in this context that the middle class began to articulate the idea of India as an independent nation-state. However, they recognized the need of a cultural project, of producing a larger 'ethnic' and cultural community, beyond the simple agenda of social and religious reform of local level religious communities. Partha Chatterjee describes this as 'classicization of tradition', which would become the foundational category of Indian nationalism. Borrowing from already available resources in orientalist and colonial representations of India, the middle class constructed India as a Hindu nation. As Chatterjee elaborates:

> A nation, or so at least the nationalist believes, must have a past. ...All that was necessary was a classicization of tradition. Orientalist scholarship had already done the groundwork for this.... The national past had been constructed by the early generation of Bengali intelligentsia as a 'Hindu' past.... This history of the nation could accommodate Islam only as a foreign element, domesticated by shearing its own lineage of a classical past. Popular Islam could then be incorporated in the national culture in the doubly sanitized form of syncretism. (Chatterjee 1993: 73–4)

While they aspired to be the natural leaders of modern India, the politics of mobilization and representation also helped the middle-class elite to pursue their 'class interests'. As Gooptu rightly points out, this politics of representation was guided by the 'need of elite politicians and leaders to negotiate with the British government for political representation or the allocation of jobs and resources; the other related to the imperatives of mass mobilization, but the two overlapped' (Gooptu 2001: 11). They often couched the demand for representation in the vocabulary of historical deprivation and economic backwardness as well as lack of political and social power and rights. Their participation in popular mobilization enabled them to reach constituencies beyond their own social rank, which in turn expanded the available public/political sphere. Newer social groups whom the middle class claimed to be representing had to become a part of the political process, giving the elite and the middle class some sort of social and political legitimacy. This legitimacy was also deployed to further their own interests to compete and lobby for government jobs and procure other benefits from the colonial state. While the middle class sought their own inclusion, their politics invariably demarcated and outlined their social status as distinct and superior to the lower caste and toiling classes.

For example, the middle-class elite shared the perception of the colonial state of the poor as a 'potential threat to political order and stability, as well as to public health and to the social or moral fabric of "respectable" urban society' (Gooptu 2001: 12), or more precisely as a 'separate social class laden with negative characteristics' (Gooptu 2001: 420). This exclusion was even more intense in the case of Dalits and the Muslim poor, who were stigmatized due to their caste and religious locations. Thus, the politics of mobilization and representation, spearheaded by the middle class, was so configured that the interests of the poor and their concerns 'deserved to be represented and furthered by the elites and political leaders. Yet, in their supposedly unreformed and unruly state, the urban poor remained effectively excluded and disenfranchised in practice from the social and political order...' (Gooptu 2001: 421).

Modernity and the Traditional Self

This new idea of India as a viable 'nation' was constructed not only in the public/political sphere but also in the private and social sphere, through a reinvention and re-articulation of 'tradition'. One of the most important concerns of the reformers was the status of women, particularly Hindu women, and family life.

Social reformers were obviously influenced and enchanted by the modern values of enlightenment, to which they were exposed during their education in English medium schools and colleges. As mediators between the colonial rulers and their own communities, they were also required to respond to what their masters saw as uncivilized practices in their communities which often involved ill-treatment of women, such as child marriage, prohibition on widow remarriage, and practices like Sati. These were identified as social evils and they needed to be curtailed, if India had to become a modern society. However, as Chaudhuri, writing about Bengal, points out, those were not the only reasons for the reformers' concern for women. They also stemmed from 'the strains that developed in the families of the newly educated men' (Chaudhuri 1993: 16). As she writes:

> The common practice for men who came to study and stayed to work in the city was to leave their families behind in the village. The tremendous gap of experience became a formidable barrier for close companionship…. The only class of women who could supply such companionship were the courtesans…. The (increasing) demand could not be met by the daughters of the traditional courtesan caste alone. The large number of young high caste widows, helpless victims of family neglect and even torture, was an obvious recruiting ground.

> Middle class social reformers concerned with the threat this posed for both the family and society, raised question about the ill treatment of widows, the denial of remarriage, child marriage and polygamy....
> (Chaudhuri 1993: 16)

It was in this context that the 'family', including women's status and their sexuality, emerged as the core concerns of middle-class social reformers. They actively collaborated with the colonial rulers in introducing various measures to ameliorate the situation. However, their efforts did not go all the way to 'liberate' women from patriarchal frames of social life. On the contrary, they passionately argued for a reassertion of tradition, which alone, they argued, could restore women's honour and the nation's identity.

Let us go back to Partha Chatterjee once again. Speaking in the same context of Bengal, Chatterjee shows how the middle-class reformers invoked a separation between the material and the spiritual in narratives through which they were working towards framing India and its distinctive identity. They accepted that the West was indeed ahead of India in science, technology, rational/modern methods of statecraft, and economic organization, and the Indians (men) had a lot to learn from them. However, they insisted that the inner sphere of home could be insulated from the Western culture by reviving the 'classical Indian tradition'. Underlying this move was the sense of anxiety of these men to protect their position of authority within the spheres of family, kinship, and caste. They argued that even though the West had progressed materially, in the inner-spiritual domain, the East was superior. This framing of separation between *ghare* (at home) and *baire* (in the outside) enabled the middle-class reformer to safely rejuvenate tradition, which had to be preserved and reproduced by women at home (*ghare*), while he himself could work hard to become modern in the outside (*baire*) world.

> ... the principal site for expressing the spiritual quality of the national culture, and women must take the main responsibility for protecting and nurturing this quality. No matter what the changes in the external conditions of life for women, they must not lose their essentially spiritual (that is, feminine) virtues; the crucial need is for the protection of the inner sanctum (Chatterjee: 1993: 126).

This had a bearing on the manner in which the idea of citizenship evolved in India. Identification of women with home and traditions also implied that they were supposed to be outside the domain of citizenship. Roy provides a useful summary of the fairly vast literature on the subject produced by historians. As she argues, while the anti-colonial nationalist ideology

> presented itself as a project of modernity dissolving ascriptive identities to constitute a unified political identity of citizen as member of a political community of equals, it remained embedded in the idea the nation as an authentic cultural tradition draws from a common past. This contradiction between the 'citizen' and the 'nation' was resolved by the nationalists through the 'natural' division of gender.

Thereby women naturally became the 'authentic "body" of the national tradition' and thus remained 'inert, backward-looking and natural'. While 'men by contrast were citizens—the agents of modernity embodying nationalism's progressive principle of rupture and change' (Roy 2014: 59).

This binary of inner and outer could not effectively work with subjects like caste, which too had come to be universally viewed as an essential element of Hindu tradition. It was hard for the middle-class reformers to deny the existence of caste because it too had been verified as an essential element of Hindu tradition by the same orientalist scholarship, from whom they had extensively borrowed, while constructing their own narrative of the glorified past of Hindu tradition.

One way out was to defend the practices of caste through a modernist and scientific logic. In his work on the Brahmins of Tamil Nadu, M.S.S. Pandian tells us:

> A number of publications in the first half of the twentieth century tried to present untouchability as a social practice based on modern rationality. These publications most often explained away untouchability by resorting to argument on hygiene and sanitation…. Hygiene and sanitation were key themes in the British medical discourse on India…. (Pandian 2007: 38)

This was done not only to establish the superiority of the upper castes as 'religious people with pure habits' over the lower castes for having 'filthy and unclean habits', but they also deployed a 'secularized language' that would validate the practice of untouchability as being a scientific and rational behaviour (Pandian 2007: 38). Further, the caste system was also presented as another form of division of labour, as a natural phenomenon in the economic evolution of societies, rather than recognizing its socio-historical specificity (Pandian 2007: 39–40).

Leadership and Hegemonic Aspirations

It is evident from the above discussion that the emergence of the middle class in India was facilitated by the colonial state through the introduction of modern education and the employment of educated Indians in offices set up for commercial, administrative, and other purposes by the colonial government (Beteille 2001). However, the colonial political policy of considering India initially as a supplier of wealth and later as a market for goods produced in Imperial Britain restricted industrial expansion in India, which in turn did not permit the significant development of an industrial middle class (managers, supervisors, and so on) (Fernandes 2006: 4).

The middle class had a contradictory political character. On one hand, as a section of colonial subjects, who acquired modern education and learnt/mastered the English language and became part of the colonial regime in various capacities, they had an inherent interest in the reproduction of 'language and colonial rule because their socio-economic and political position rested on social, cultural and economic capital associated with colonial education, training and state employment' (Fernandes 2006: 5). On the other hand, these Western/modern educated Indians were also inspired by the political ideas of self-rule, liberty, and freedom, which eventually formed the bedrock of the struggle for self-determination against colonial rule (Alavi 1975: 1237).

Further, the middle class had two interrelated roles that shaped their political character vis-à-vis the colonial state and market. Notwithstanding their other social identities (of caste, community, and in some cases, even aristocratic status), members of the middle class developed a self-image of being progressive Indians, who had the legitimate right to represent interests of the subject population, as leaders of the common masses. Quite early in its history, the Indian middle class began to develop, what Fernandes and Heller call 'hegemonic aspirations' (2006).

Unlike its Western counterpart who claimed the position of leadership in society by actively pursuing a politics of citizenship for all, the Indian middle class did so by actively pursuing a sectarian agenda, even when it invoked a universalistic and modern language. Through its discursive practices, it tried to reinforce women's subordination through reviving, inventing, and consolidating the idea of Indian tradition. In the process, it also pushed the Muslims and the Dalits to margins of the emerging Indian society because the glorious tradition that it invested and celebrated was by definition an upper-caste Hindu tradition. Being middle class enabled it to position itself away from all other 'identities'.

However, the idea of the universality of the middle class was also fluid and acquired differing articulations depending on the context. The universal identity was actively deployed while seeking political freedom. However, while competing for specific economic and political benefits from the colonial masters, particularistic identities of community and religion were emphasized, including things like numerical strength vis-à-vis other communities.

To realize its hegemonic aspirations, the middle class also tried to frame a politics of respectability. The politics of respectability defined the norms of socially acceptable behaviour in the public sphere. The poor were seen as continuously transcending the limits of acceptable social behaviour and hence there was a call for morally and socially disciplining them (Gooptu 2001; Kidambi 2012) or to set a physical limit on their movement in urban spaces.

3

The Age of Development and Nation Building

Freedom and power bring responsibility…. The service of India means the service of the millions who suffer. It means the ending of poverty and ignorance and disease and inequality of opportunity. The ambition of the greatest man of our generation has been to wipe every tear from every eye…. And so we have to labour and to work and work hard to give reality to our dreams.[1]

[1] The speech, famously called 'Tryst with Destiny', by Jawaharlal Nehru, the first Prime Minister of independent India, to the Indian Constituent Assembly in the Parliament, on the eve of India's Independence, towards midnight on 14 August 1947. (Available at http://www.svc.ac.in/files/TRYST%20WITH%20DESTINY.pdf [accessed on 5 November 2014].)

These words of Nehru, spoken in sophisticated English, at the time of India's independence from colonial rule in 1947, were clearly addressed to the fellow political elite and the English-speaking middle classes of India, who, along with him, had the capacity and responsibility of developing the newly liberated country and building it into a viable nation-state. The enormous task of ushering in social and economic 'growth with equity' rested on the shoulders of the 'enlightened' and the 'educated' professionals, bureaucrats, and intellectuals. They alone were imbued with scientific temper and rational minds to carry forward the historical mandate and ensure 'that this ancient land attain her rightful place in the world and make her full and willing contribution to the promotion of world peace and the welfare of mankind'.[2]

At the time of its independence, India faced many challenges. Colonial rule had been a source of many problems and contradictions. While it facilitated some kind of modern industrialization, it also left India's economy, particularly its agrarian economy that supported more than three-fourths of its population, in

---

[2] 'Tryst with Destiny'.

shatters. Rural settlements in most of the subcontinent, where 9 out of 10 Indians lived at that time, remained deeply unequal and hierarchical, segmented along the axes of caste, class, and community. Even though an indigenous class of private industrialists and business-men had grown during the later decades of colonial rule, their social base, vision, and impact remained very limited. Even when it introduced secular education, which gave birth to a new mobile and modern middle class, and set up new institutions of governance that brought about some kind of administrative unification, the Hindu–Muslim communal divide grew, eventu-ally resulting in the bloody Partition that left millions homeless and many dead. Such contradictions emerged in other spheres of Indian life as well.

The nationalist political elite that took over the reigns of power from the colonial rulers knew of these challenges. Perhaps the most immediate task before the new political establishment was to expand its capac-ity by establishing institutions that would work in different spheres of national life: social, political, and economic. The Indian state invested heavily in all these spheres. A direct implication of this state-led expansion of economic and governance spheres was a gradual, but significant, expansion of the middle class, both in numbers as well as in influence.

As the state expanded its spheres of activity and invested in building infrastructure for economic growth, it added to the numbers of middle-class Indians simply by adding personnel on its roles. Besides the state bureaucracy and economic planning, the middle class also increased in numbers with expanding media, modern education, and other activities—private and public—in the growing metropolis. The state invested a great deal of money in setting up colleges and universities, institutions of specialized learning to produce specialized human resources, scientific capabilities, and modern infrastructure. The expansion of the state and its institutions as the primary vehicle for socio-economic transformation of an underdeveloped nation directly benefited the middle classes. These educated middle classes became the agents and bearers of modernity. Middle-class expansion among different sections of the Indian population also became a source of legitimacy for the Indian state. They became its mouthpiece and active advocates of its policies.

Middle-Class Imaginations of a Modern India

India was not the only country that acquired independence from colonial rule. The Second World War had considerably weakened the colonial powers. Given their own compulsions, many of them chose to withdraw from direct control over their colonies. Powerful nationalist movements also made it difficult for the empires to sustain their control over the colonies.

While the political leaders of many poor countries of the newly emergent Third World were attracted to the revolutionary doctrine of socialism developed by Karl Marx and others for restructuring social and economic life in their societies, the middle classes generally preferred simple 'evolutionary models', presented in the then popular dualistic and modernization theories of economic and social change made popular by social scientists from the United States. These theories proposed a simple model of social transformation, which required the Third World countries to imitate the West, inculcate 'modern' values, develop modern institutions as they had come up in the West and lay modern infrastructure for rapid industrialization that would enable the rural population to move to urban centres.

The dominant political spectrum under the leadership of Jawaharlal Nehru, actively supported by the native industrial class, the bourgeoisie, wanted India to become a modern country, like those in the West. The newly emergent middle-class Indians also aspired for a modern life, similar to the life in a Western city. They were the ones who had worked with the Congress party in its struggle for independence. The middle class also spoke on behalf of the large masses of the subcontinent. As Khilnani rightly argues:

> Nationalism was the politics of an urban educated elite that presumed itself entitled to negotiate with the British and speak on behalf of the country's villages. For the early nationalist generations, independence meant being free to emulate colonial city life, it promised the opportunity to take up addresses in the residential sanctuary of the civil lines, to create a world where public trees would flourish unabused. (Khilnani 1997: 125)

After Independence, they also argued for their way of taking the country forward, through writings and political campaigns. The idea of planning for development evolved out of such an imagination, an outcome of the collaboration between the political elite of independent India, its nascent bourgeoisie, and its middle-class elite.

One of the first detailed articulations of this could be found in the writings of an accomplished engineer from south India, M. Visvesvaraya, who was the Diwan of the Mysore state. He had designed drinking water and sanitary systems of many cities including both Hyderabad and Karachi. He also established systems of flood control in Orissa and was instrumental in planning the generation of electricity in Mysore. He was associated with the Tata Iron and Steel Company in Jamshedpur as well. In his book called *Planned Economy for India* (1936), he proposed a model of nation building, which was to be carried out by India's educated middle class. He explicitly advocated a capitalist economy along the lines of the European and US economies. He advocated rapid industrialization based on mechanization, especially heavy industries, those relating to the manufacture of machinery and heavy chemicals. Traditional agriculture and its accompanying cottage industries could not take India very far, he argued (Visvesvaraya 1936; Vyasulu 1989). Nation building was closely linked to a desire to catch up with the 'rapid changes taking place in methods of production, means of locomotion and business practices in the *civilized world*' (Visvesvaraya 1936: 165, emphasis ours).

However, unlike the Western countries, he underlined the need for planned economic development in India through a 'central economic council' entrusted with the task of preparing a proposal for a ten-year plan and its subsequent operation. The central economic council, in his view, was to be constituted by drawing in 50 experts comprising 'mainly of economists and leading business men representing the various organizations and activities in all parts of the country in agriculture, industries, commerce, transport, banking and finance' (Visvesvaraya 1936: 180). Only a planned economy could ensure the rapid advance of industry, agriculture, commerce, and finance particularly for increasing production, reducing unemployment, and greater interdependence between the various parts of India. It would help in training the required human resource in the practical arts of business and administration (Visvesvaraya: 1936: 146). The role of the government, for him, was to create conditions for capitalist development in India. The state ought to provide banking and credit facilities and adequate tariff controls. Interestingly, his model of development asked for a strong bureaucracy that would enforce economic discipline and maintain law and order. He was also among the first to advocate a scientifically defined poverty line and minimum wages.

Even though he did not directly visualize any role for the middle class, his model essentially proposed state supported capitalist development with a strong middle class facilitating and administering it. He wrote on the critical need for developing middle-class sensibilities through 'Training for Business Life and Citizenship' (Visvesvaraya: 1936: 165–77). Modern citizenship required a certain kind of civility and participation in the economic life of the nation. Visvesvaraya firmly believed that India lacked these conditions. Therefore, he advocated building up a 'new outlook in life' where 'people are literate, active and efficient and are imbued with progressive ideals'. The outdated customs and traditions were restraining growth of individualism that would enable Indians to develop the capacity to 'prosper on their own'. Only an educated workforce could contribute towards *national efficiency* and *individual efficiency*.

Interestingly, India's business leaders of that time also proposed a similar model for India's development through a document published in 1944, called 'Memorandum Outlining a Plan of Economic Development for India', popularly known as the 'Bombay Plan'. Its authors were the top business elite of the time and included J.R.D. Tata, G.D. Birla, Sir Ardeshir Dalal, Sir Shri Ram, Kasturbhai Lalbhai, A.D. Shroff, and John Matthai. The chief proposals of the memorandum were as follows: centralized planning for the entire economy; economic controls in order to pull India out of the clutches of economic backwardness and low level of growth; a concentrated programme of heavy industry in the public sector; and deficit financing so as to finance the various aspects of the plan such as education, health, and housing, raising agricultural and industrial output (Thakurdas et al. 1944).

The Bombay Plan also flagged a few critical problems and suggested corresponding remedial interventions, which by implication was to enable expansion in middle-class numbers. It proposed an increase in the total national income, and reduction of economic disparities, which would increase the per capita incomes of common citizens. Towards this goal, the plan favoured a combination of state initiative and market-based solutions. It argued for the creation of basic heavy industry in the public sector including infrastructure services like power, railways, roads, and shipping. It advocated encouraging private enterprise, but it also recognized the need of pulling people out of low incomes and poverty, and propelling an appreciable number of them towards middle-class status, a task that only an economically active state could perform. It proposed a target of reducing dependence on agriculture and increasing employment in industry and the service sector at a rapid pace.

As has been pointed out by students of contemporary Indian history, the political establishment under the leadership of Jawaharlal Nehru eventually chose a model of modernizing and developing India that favoured industrial growth over the Gandhian model of village-centric reforms. As is well known, Gandhi, the most prominent leader of India's freedom struggle, was opposed to such a model of social change. For him true freedom, *swaraj*, lay in recovering and reconstructing the traditional village, harmonious and self-contained, uncorrupted by the modern life of the city and Western technology. It was only through the reconstruction of the village that India could recover its lost self. Even though Gandhi was the tallest leader of India's freedom movement, his viewpoint of creating a federal polity based upon the self-organizing capacity of the Indian village was consciously rejected (Mantena 2012: 536). In contrast, Visvesvaraya's ideas had a significant influence. This resulted in the adoption of what has come to be known as the Nehru–Mahalanobis Model of economic change (Vyasulu 1989). Similarly, the idea of a developmental state proposed by the Bombay Plan was incorporated in the Industrial Policy Statement (Chibber 2003: 94–104).

The relevant broad contours of the Nehru–Mahalanobis model were as follows:

1. The government and/or the 'public sector' should be responsible for developing heavy industries like mining, metals, and machine-building industries. This required a disproportionate investment in machine-building complexes.

2. Economic independence and self-reliance was identified with the creation of heavy industrialization, which the colonial regime had not developed.

3. Emphasis on heavy industry would produce shortfall in consumer goods, which was to be taken care of by the expansion of cottage and small-scale industries.

4. Besides fulfilling the need of providing locally produced cheap consumer goods, this sector was to also generate employment and help develop a large class of new entrepreneurs.

5. Heavy industrialization was also to enable growth of agriculture by providing locally made modern equipment, thus helping mechanize and modernize cultivation (Mahalanobis 1955; Joshi 1979; Chibber 2003; Balakrishnan 2007).

Unlike the state-controlled socialist economies of the erstwhile communist countries like the Soviet Union, the planned economic development of India was to be carried out within the political framework of a liberal democracy. Industrialization was not only an instrument to spearhead economic growth but was also seen as an institution that could positively influence the socio-economic fabric. The process of industrialization, according to this view, was capable of fundamentally denting the regressive social and economic structures and could help equalize wealth and income in rural areas, loosen the traditional caste ties, which may in turn also promote inter-religious and inter-caste marriages (Bayly 2012). In short the economic framework of development coupled with representative democracy was expected to usher in social, cultural, and economic modernization of India.

Planning and the Middle-Class Expansion

Modern institutions in the realm of the economy and polity were to pull the nation out of social obscurantism, challenge social hierarchies, and enable fast-paced economic development. This was a model of nation building that required the creation of a new institutional framework to be staffed by educated and technically skilled Indians, those from the existing educated middle classes, but also many first generation migrants from rural areas, who were able to get into the expanding network of educational institutions.

The first three or four decades of economic growth, popularly called the Nehruvian phase of development planning, saw a massive expansion of Indian capabilities in the field of science and technology, in state supported industry, and in bureaucratic structures. Interestingly, as discussed in the previous chapter, under British colonial rule, the subcontinent had already witnessed the emergence of a few significant urban centres of governance systems and institutions of Western style secular education. A small section of urban population was exposed to Western/modern ideas and modes of organizing economic and political systems as they had evolved in the West. The independent Indian state continued with most of the civil and criminal administrative systems instituted by the colonial rulers, but with an added strength of nationalist legitimacy, presented as being critical for nation building and the development of the Indian people.

In the context of our discussion, this implied retaining the older bureaucracy, recruited by the colonial state, but also its manifold expansion. As the state created newer institutions and expanded its reach to different corners of the country, the number of people serving in these institutions also increased. Planning for development and its delivery also required a new kind of bureaucracy, which was development oriented and could usher in not only economic changes but also guide it as per the social and political priorities of the independent Indian state.

This development bureaucracy was broadly divided between the elite Indian Administrative Services (IAS), central government services at the federal level, and provincial civil services at the state level. They were to carry forward the mandate of their respective ministries and departments headed by the political executive. Besides, the strength of a large number of specialized offices, old and new, expanded over the years. These included judiciary, commissions, and technical training institutions. The authorized cadre strength of the Indian Administrative Service was merely 1,232 in the year 1951 to which 532 officers were added during the first decade after Independence. Their numbers steadily increased in the subsequent years and by the end of the 1980s there were 5,334 sanctioned IAS posts (GOI 2012: 46).

In due course the ministries and departments established a large number of public sector organizations to further the developmental mandate. They covered almost every sector of the emerging Indian economy: finance, heavy engineering, heavy metals, chemicals and fertilizers, manufacturing, services, transport, agro-based industries, medium and light engineering, transport, power and energy, petroleum, mining, textiles, and even hotels. Big public sector organizations were viewed as being critical for unfolding of the Nehruvian model of development and their numbers grew quite rapidly during the first two decades after Independence. During this period India also initiated construction of several large scale river valley hydropower projects. Nehru had famously (or infamously!) described them as 'temples of modern India'. They were to be the foundation for building a self-reliant India, a source of energy and water for land. Besides, India also initiated several ports and port services augmenting facilities within the framework of the public sector. Several of the existing ports at Bombay, Chennai, Visakhapatnam, and Mormugão were further expanded.

In addition to investments in building capacity for hydropower, the Nehruvian state also set up the National Coal Development Corporation (NCDC) in 1956. With the exception of the coal mines owned by the Tatas and a few others, all the coal mines were declared as national resources, effectively owned by the Government of India. Likewise, the Industrial Policy Resolution of 1956 placed the mineral oil industry in the Schedule-A list of industries, which made further developments in this sector as the sole and exclusive responsibility of the state. Accordingly, the Oil and Natural Gas Commission (ONGC) (1959) was given the sole right to 'plan, promote, organize and implement programmes for development of petroleum resources and the production and sale of petroleum and petroleum products produced by it, and to perform such other functions as the Central Government may, from time to time, assign to it'.[3] It promoted public sector units, such as, the Indian Oil Corporation, Bharat Petroleum, and Hindustan Petroleum Corporations. State level electricity boards and road transport corporations were formed during the 1960s.

All these organizations were to hire a large number of educated and skilled workers, who were to be

[3] See the short official history of ONGC (1947–60), available at http://ongcindia.ongc.co.in/wps/wcm/connect/ongcindia/Home/Company/History/ (accessed on 13 February 2015)

TABLE 3.1 Public and Private Sector Organized Employment (in millions)

	Public Sector*	Private Sector
1956	5.23	NA
1961	7.05	5.05
1965	8.95	6.04
1970	10.33	6.73
1975	13.63	6.79
1980	15.48	7.24

Source: *Economic Survey*, Ministry of Finance–GOI, 1971 and *RBI Handbook of Statistics*, 2000.
Note: *Public Sector includes, central, state, local, and quasi government.

the expanding middle class of India. The Nehruvian state also set up organizations that were to facilitate the creation of such human resources for the expanding needs of the country. These included the Indian Institute of Management (IIMs), Indian Institute of Technology (IITs) and a large network of laboratories under the Council of Scientific and Industrial Research (CSIR). The Indian Council for Agriculture Research was further expanded. The Tata Institute of Fundamental Research, originally started with support from Sir Dorabji Tata Trust in 1945, was also expanded with support from the Government of India in 1954. Similarly, the University Grant Commission (UGC) was set up in 1956 as a 'statutory body' for 'the coordination, determination and maintenance of standards of university education in India'. The number of universities and colleges expanded rapidly. In the year 1950–1 India had 370 colleges in general education, 208 for professional education, and 27 universities. By the end of 1980 their numbers had gone up to 3,421 colleges for general education, 3,542 colleges for professional education, and 110 universities/deemed universities. The number of students they all trained also rose manifold.

During the period of 15 years, from 1956 to 1970, the state sector added 5.10 million workers. In the next one decade, the growth was even more impressive and nearly the same numbers were added to organized public sector employment (see Table 3.1).

Even the private sector that grew during this period partially depended on the state system for its growth. Many ancillary industries that came up in the private sector were to feed the large public sector units. Similarly, expanding employment in the public sector provided a boost to markets of various kinds, promoting a new generation of entrepreneurs. These ancillary economic activities also contributed to the growth of the middle classes and middle-income populations. During 1960s and 1970s, a total of 1.7 million new workers were added.

The spurt in economic activity created a need for the expansion of the railways, banking, and postal services. The Indian Railways started its organizational journey in 1853 with a train connecting Bombay with Thane, a stretch of 21 miles, and the first passenger train was between Howrah and Hooghly, covering a distance of 24 miles. Over the years, Indian Railways witnessed massive expansion. Though it was first started to serve the economic interests of the colonial master as mentioned earlier, it evolved into a significant institution for transportation as well as for the socio-economic development of India after its independence (Alivelu 2010: 5). In 1951, the Indian railways lifted 37,565 million net tons kilometre (NTKM)[4] of freight traffic while undertaking 66,517 million passenger

---

[4] Net ton kilometres is the number of tons of freight carried multiplied by the average distance over which it is transported.

kilometres (PKM).[5] By the year 1980–1 the NTKM and PKM stood at 147,652 and 208,558 millions respectively. The contribution of the Indian Railways in developing, adding, and sustaining the educated (lower) middle class is also quite significant. In the year 1950–1, Indian Railways employed 2,300 Group A and B (management personnel) officers, 223,500 Group C, and 687,800 Group D workers. By the end of 1980, it employed 112,000 Group A and B Officers, while Group C and D employees stood at 721,100 and 839,900 respectively.

The history of the Indian banking system during the post-Independence period has been a little complicated; nevertheless, the number of people working in the system saw a manifold increase during the period, particularly after major commercial banks were nationalized by the central government led by Indira Gandhi. In the year 1969, there were 89 commercial banks (72 scheduled commercial banks and 17 non-scheduled commercial banks). By the end of 1989, the number

[5] Passenger kilometres are defined as total number of passengers multiplied by the average distance over which they travel.

had gone up to 278, out of which 196 were Regional Rural Banks and 4 were non-scheduled commercial banks. With an expanding network of branches in different parts of the country, the strength of the Banking staff grew several folds. In the year 1969, the banking system in the country had 8,162 officers, 26,122 clerks, and 11,707 other subordinate staff. By 1989, there were 43,621 officers, 83,916 clerks, and 36,375 directly working in the banks as subordinate officers.

The primary emphasis of Nehruvian development planning remained on industrialization. However, Indian agriculture, albeit in some regions, also developed quite rapidly, particularly after the relatively successful adoption of the Green Revolution technology during the late 1960s and later. The droughts of 1965–6 and 1966–7 and the resultant food insecurity led to surging import bills on food items and reliance on food imports from the United States (US) under its Public Law (PL) 480 initiative, which meant to tackle world's hunger. However, the US government demanded that in return India conform to US policies in the Third World. It was in this context that the Government of India initiated new programmes of agricultural development by expanding irrigation capacity through the lifting of ground water and introduction of high-yielding variety (HYV) seeds.

This was supplemented by public investment in rural roads and a system of procurement prices that greatly reduced uncertainty for farmers, thereby motivating them to grow more food. Rural Electrification Corporation (REC) was established in the public sector in the year 1969. The REC along with the Agriculture Refinance Corporation (established in 1963) and commercial banks provided loans to state electricity boards. Almost 1.25 million pump sets and tube wells were energized between 1966 and 1969. The National Thermal Power Corporation (NTPC) was also set up in 1975 to help meet the power demand required for intensive irrigation.

These initiatives proved to be quite successful and by the 1970s the Indian countryside in the Green Revolution pockets began to change socially, economically, and politically. A new class of surplus producing farmers emerged on the scene. This class of 'gentleman farmers' (Thorner 1969) was to increasingly become integrated with the urban market and social life. Not only did they sell their surplus farm produce to urban traders and government procurement agencies and buy farm inputs, but also sent their children for urban education, who in turn eventually aspired for an urban middle-class life (see Jodhka 2014).

Despite a relatively slow growth rate and many challenges and frequent 'crises' of various kinds, the Indian economy witnessed a significant expansion during the first three or four decades after Independence, thanks largely to the active role of the Indian state. Most of this happened with the expansion of its bureaucratic systems and investments in public sector establishments and through its initiatives that enabled agriculture and other economic activities to grow. The growth of the middle class during this period was not only substantive in terms of numbers; it also created grounds for the next phase of its expansion in the subsequent decades, particularly during the post-1990s period.

4

Transforming India, from Above

The development state was seen primarily as an engine of production... But the ideological justification of this constantly expanding state machinery was in terms of arguments of distributive justice.... The state sector came to control vast economic resources—through its gigantic, interconnected networks of financing, employment, and contracts emanating from both the productive and welfare activities of the state enterprises.... The huge economic bureaucracy of the developmental state increasingly had little to do with realistic distributive policies, but became utterly dependent on a disingenuous use of that rhetoric. (Kaviraj 2010: 224–5)

As we have discussed in the previous chapter, after its independence from colonial rule, India embarked upon a journey of change with hopes and aspirations. The new 'native' leaders, who inherited power from the colonial rulers, chose a model of politics that was to take the country forward on a path of development and progress and make India a modern society. While it underlined the need for individual freedom, including the freedom to own private capital, it also aspired for a social change that would usher in a new culture of citizenship and reduce persistent inequalities. Even though a section of its political elite was attracted to socialism, India chose a capitalist model of economic growth with an active role for the state. The state was to actively participate in laying the economic foundations for India's industrial growth by investing in the development of infrastructure and heavy industries that required large volumes of investment.

Through its proactive policies, the Indian state was also to work for building a new India that would care for its poor and enable them to enhance their capacities of participation in the national social, economic, and political life. Even though some scholars have argued that through state planning the Indian state intended to lay the foundation of a socialist type of economy (Rao 1982; Kohli 2011: 12–13), a closer examination would show that the main objective of state intervention in India's economy was to lay the foundation of a liberal capitalist economy (Byres 1997).

The political elite of the time realized that if a capitalist economy and liberal democracy had to grow in India, they needed to initiate measures to weaken the stranglehold of 'feudal' patriarchs over its rural/agrarian economy and society that had become even stronger under colonial rule. Soon after Independence, the state governments were directed by the central government to initiate legislative measures through a variety of Land Reform legislations to incentivize the effective tillers of land and give them ownership rights by abolishing 'semi-feudal' intermediaries. In the political sphere it meant establishing institutions for democratic governance, providing a constitutional guarantee of equality to all citizens irrespective of their social location, and programmes for capability enhancement of poor and historically marginalized social groups, conceived and implemented by a huge developmental administration. The new Constitution of the Indian republic abolished untouchability and institutionalized quotas for historically deprived groups in state-run educational institutions and in employment in state-owned institutions/enterprises. Given its size and diversity, these were mammoth tasks to be carried out within the framework of a liberal democratic institutional order.

As we have discussed in the previous chapter, in order to fulfill these promises, the new developmental state required the services of a large number of people who were not only educated and skilled but also had the mind-set and orientation required for such a project of nation building. Thus, quite like the colonial state, the developmental state was also confronted with the need to create a new middle class. However, this time the middle class had to have a different orientation and social composition. The new political elite of India decided to produce such a class through an expansion of education and training within the country. This process of formal education was to help citizens enhance their economic entrepreneurship and develop their faculties of reason and imaginative thinking, making them capable of participating and helping the state in the processes of growth and development administration. It also implied creating policy frameworks for erecting economic institutions that could redress poverty and economic backwardness and facilitate the social and economic mobility of diverse categories of people.

The nationalist middle-class elite that emerged during the colonial period were not averse to tradition or religious beliefs. In fact, as we have seen in Chapter 2, many of them had actively participated in religious reforms that also produced a new imagination of their own communitarian selves. However, there was a virtual consensus among the new leaders of independent India that the process of economic growth and spread of modern political institutions would inevitably dissolve regressive social features emanating from past tradition—the caste system and the other similar social institutions.

The new rulers of India firmly believed that the country would enthusiastically move towards embracing the idea of equal citizenship where every individual is valued for his/her inherent worth. As the change in economic order progressed, the privileges and disabilities inherited from the past and/or social origin would begin to matter less and less. In a move away from the caste system, social interactions and economic exchanges would no longer be governed by custom and traditional norms. Nor would emergent political and economic systems be embedded in the social framework of caste. On the contrary, as was believed to be the case with other modern societies, the social interactions in India would begin to be dictated by the norms of modern economy, secular values, and democratic political system. This was not simply wishful thinking on the part of the modern leadership of the country but also a part of its agenda and promise to the nation, on the basis of which it claimed legitimacy for itself (Austin 1966; Kothari 1970; Rudolph and Rudolph 1987; Khilnani 1997).

Even though the business elite and agrarian rich had considerable influence over the emerging political order, the Indian middle class also occupied a critical position in shaping and articulating the politics and policies of the times. The Indian middle class was literally placed in the middle of the new regime, between the rulers and the traditional rich on one side and the so-called common people on the other. Most interestingly, it was through these policies and initiatives of the new regime that the 'middle' in India was to undergo a considerable expansion in size and influence. The colonial middle class was largely made up of a small number of professionals, who mostly came from socially privileged backgrounds. As we have seen in the previous chapter, the new regime expanded the size of its bureaucracy manifold and made large investments in setting up a variety of institutions and economic enterprises, which increased the size of the Indian middle class. This expanding middle class was in turn to become the social and economic base of the emerging capitalist economy. The process of economic development was to expand the Indian economy and provide impetus to the growth of a variety of diverse occupations and newer lower middle classes, which were to add diversity to the existing middle class.

The Age of Nehruvian Developmentalism

The first three or four decades after India's independence were marked by a kind of continuity in economic policy and political orientation. They were geared towards translating the vision of India's first prime minister, Pandit Jawaharlal Nehru, into practice. Even though the Indian economy did not grow very rapidly, it underwent significant changes through a gradual process of industrialization, agrarian change, and considerable expansion of a variety of infrastructure. The idea of 'planning for development' remained a dominant approach to economic policy. Democracy too survived. With the exception of a brief period of Emergency during the 1970s, India continued to elect its governments, central and federal, at regular intervals.

Even though the middle class grew in size and influence, the source of its power was largely through its mediating role in executing state initiatives. From formulating planning documents and managing educational institutions to running state-supported hospitals or helping farmers in growing new crops and use of fertilizers, this middle class worked on several fronts. It had a mission to work as an agency of India's modernization and development.

Notwithstanding their diverse social and cultural backgrounds, they viewed their role towards the nation and society with a sense of idealism and high-minded purpose transcending purely individual concerns. They were a typically salaried and professional class, without any direct creative involvement in trade, commerce, and industry. Given that they mostly worked within the state system or its allied institutions, their salaries were not very high, particularly in comparison to international standards. However, their influence was significant or, as Mazzarella puts it, they were 'short on money but long on institutional perks' (2004: 1).

While its members occupied critical positions in the political system and development regime, other interests and actors active on different economic and political fronts of Indian society limited their influence. Until around the 1980s, agrarian economies of many states and regions in India were still controlled by traditional landlords from dominant and upper castes. Not only did they remain powerful in the rural settings of their territorial regions, they often also dictated the directions of economic and social change. Interestingly, even though democratic and electoral politics was formally institutionalized, it only helped these interests to consolidate their hold over regional politics, at least during the first three or four decades after the introduction of electoral politics (Frankel and Rao 1989).

What role did this Nehruvian middle class play during these decades of economic planning? Did it actually work as an active and positive agency in nation building, enabling the process of development and state-service delivery? Or did it only help the new ruling elite, agrarian rich and business interests, to consolidate their position in independent India through providing legitimacy to their growing influence in the name of development? Or was it simply focused on itself, self-serving, power hungry, and narrow minded?

There is an iota of truth in all these characterizations of the middle class of those decades. However, the critical point is that India could not have moved ahead during this period without expanding its middle classes. To help its economy grow, its backward agriculture and nascent industry to grow; to develop its diverse regions/communities and provide them with education, health care, and security; to manage its vast territories through institutionalizing democratic process and bureaucratic delivery system, India had to expand its middle classes. India's growth story over the years clearly shows that this new middle class played a positive role in nation building. They were also required for Indian democracy to flourish. It is mostly from their ranks and files that new generations of leaders emerged who articulated the interests and aspirations of different regions and communities and helped in the process of negotiated development.

However, as the Marxist scholars would argue, these middle-class individuals worked within the state system, as per the directives of their masters. They had to often accommodate the locally powerful and the larger economic interests of India's new ruling classes. Though there were many instances where an individual member of the bureaucracy or an independent professional would challenge vested class interests of the rulers and align with those at the receiving-end in the system, their numbers were often small.

As individuals and members of communities and associations, they also had their private and personal interests to serve. As Chatterjee rightly points out, the Nehruvian middle class saw itself 'as the universal class, satisfying in the service of the state its private interest by working for the universal goal of the nation' (Chatterjee 1997: 88). Unlike some other countries, the state system in India enjoyed a considerable degree of autonomy from the dominant class interests (see Kohli 1987; Rudolph and Rudolph 1987). Even though most of the discretionary powers of the Indian state system lay ultimately with the elected representative, members of the bureaucracy also enjoyed significant amount of power over these resources. Some scholars have also pointed to the fact that during this period, India did not have a single powerful class. Thanks to the implementation of Land Reform legislations and powerful agrarian movements of the poor in some regions, old feudal interests were dwindling while industrial capitalism was still in its early stages of growth (Bardhan 1984; Vanaik 1990). The growing needs of skilled and educated personnel in a developing economy like India also worked as a source of influence and power for the middle classes (Rudra 1989).

Dispositions and Self-Interest

As the state's development role expanded, so did the size, influence, power, and geographical spread of this middle class. Quite like its ancestor, the colonial middle class, this category of Indians also had their share of contradictory dispositions. Given that a large majority of them came from relatively privileged backgrounds—the upper castes and dominant communities of the diverse Indian society—they invariably had their own biases and opinions. While they were happy to embrace modernity, they were not always comfortable with growing demands for inclusion from below through the dynamics of 'democracy'. Even though this class was a product of modernity and often deployed the language of universal state, development, and democracy, its own social base was quite narrow. In other words, its attitude towards universal citizenship was, at best, ambivalent. Dipankar Gupta is perhaps right when he critiques the Indian middle class as being weak in 'its commitment to principles of democracy' and strong in its dependence 'on connections, family and patronage' (Gupta 2000: 9).

Another famous commentator on the Indian middle class, Pavan Varma, is even more critical of its self-serving attitude and indifference toward the poor. As he writes:

In an interventionist state in a poor economy, those who control state power tend to exercise enormous influence, and in newly independent India, the upper and middle classes were the most strategically placed to control state power. Their representatives ran the all-powerful bureaucracy, they were fully represented in the legislature; they were at the helm of business and industry; they had an outlet for their views in the media; and in the countryside they owned most of the land. The result was that the interests of the middle class hijacked the agenda of the nation, even as its members continued to believe that the State was rightly biased in favour of the less privileged. (Varma 1998: 50)

Given that Nehruvian India also worked proactively to protect its nascent industry from global competition, it also put in place a rigorous regime of licenses and quotas to discourage the growth of economic monopolies. These policies gave additional power to those in the bureaucracy, state controlled commercial banks, and other such intermediaries. These could become sources of unlimited power, often leading to corrupt practices that favoured a select few. Prem Shankar Jha goes to the extent of arguing that 'since this class benefitted from economic controls, it could perpetuate and even strengthen the regime of shortages' (Jha 1980: viii), which gave it greater discretionary powers. The Indian state, with its massive infrastructure and the legitimacy to penetrate every aspect of society and economy, provided the means to members of the middle class to use such a position to their advantage. The source of its influence and power during this period was primarily because of its proximity to the state system.

While there is an element of truth in this, such arguments also have their limitations. They tend to work with a singular notion of the Indian middle class and ignore its plural and particularistic locations. The Indian middle class has never been a homogenous category. With the manifold expansion during this period, its heterogeneity grew further. This heterogeneity is not merely based on the variety of economic locations that its members occupy but also on the diverse social and historical identities of region, religion, gender, ethnicity, caste, and community of its members. Given that the independent Indian state also initiated policies like reservations for Scheduled Castes (SCs) and Scheduled Tribes (STs) and universalized democratic systems of governance, the diversity of the middle class became even more critical.

This is also true for gender. Even though we do not have any numbers and their overall representation remains far below their proportions in the population, the number of women in middle-class occupations has been steadily growing during the post-Independence period. This is true not only about government jobs, but also about middle-class professions such as medicine, teaching, and law.

Even though the popular feminist view would tend to look at the state initiative for development as being gender blind, at least during the early years of development planning, the Indian state surprisingly had a rather clear view on the subject. Leaders of the nationalist movement appointed a Sub-committee as a part of the National Planning Committee as early as 1939. The committee had 27 members, all women. Unlike social reformers of the 19th century, members of the Sub-committee viewed the women's question from a citizenship perspective. As Chaudhuri writes:

> The terms of reference ... laid emphasis on providing equal opportunity as a matter right of enable her to take 'full share in India's planned economy'. Entry into the production sphere was seen as the key to resolving the unequal status of women. This is a radical departure from the concern of 19th century reformers and early nationalists with middle class women's issues stemming wholly from their lives within the family. (Chaudhuri 1995: 213–14)

Commenting on another important report commissioned by the Indian state system and produced by a group of women activists, Towards Equality, in the

1970s, Mary John also highlights the women activists' perspective on women's equality being engaged through the provisions of the Indian Constitution and the agenda of nation building, and not through the categories of Western feminism (John 1996). The rise of women's movements during the 1970s and 1980s was already a reflection of the growing size of middle-class women in the urban public sphere, particularly in educational institutions at different levels.

Any formulation on the middle class has to examine this fluidity and recognize the significance of particularistic identities while still retaining the elements of some form of commonality of identity. However, this is not to suggest that during this period the Indian middle class had indeed acquired a representative national character. On the contrary, despite growing diversities, social bases of the dominant or the 'mainstream' middle class has remained rather narrow.

For example, it is a well-known fact that the Indian bureaucracy has mostly been populated by select upper castes in each region. For instance, in Uttar Pradesh, Kayasthas, Brahmins, and Thakurs have been numerically preponderant at almost all levels of the bureaucratic hierarchy. Similarly, Kayasthas and Brahmins have tended to dominate the officialdom of West Bengal while members of the locally dominant communities of Vokkaliga and Lingayats have had a major share of bureaucratic positions in the state of Karnataka. Similar trends have been present in most other states/regions of the country as well.

More importantly, sections within such middle-class locations tend also to deploy their particularistic identities, of caste and community, in competitive situations. They form 'lobbies' on caste lines, which promote and favour their own members for plum postings and transfers, eventually reinforcing the power of the dominant castes at the regional level. Similarly, Francine Frankel (1978) shows how the complex interaction between democratic politics, national and state political leaders, and members of the dominant castes in rural areas produces a specific kind of alliance. Such networks also shape the politics of patronage and 'clientelism' at the regional level.

Interestingly, this active involvement of middle-class individuals with their community-based associations further reinforced the power of the state official. Such politics of patronage extended to the discretionary powers of the individual bureaucrats through their control over subsidy dispensing machinery (also noted by Bardhan 1984). The expansion of the subsidy regime and consequent economic benefits strengthened the big farmers economically and further bolstered their social identities through their perceived power and domination over electoral processes in the rural hinterlands. Such subsidies were not limited to agricultural inputs but also extended to cooperatives, non-farm sector initiatives, and small-scale industries.

These complex dynamics of social and economic mobility at the local level and its interaction with the developmental state and its selective patronage has over the years produced a class of rural rich, big and medium landowners belonging to specific caste communities, such as the Jats in western Uttar Pradesh, Punjab, and Haryana, the Maratha sugarcane farmers in Maharashtra, the Pattidar Patels in Gujarat, and the Reddys and Kammas in Andhra Pradesh. The source of their power and dominance does not emanate merely from their dominance in agrarian economy but increasingly also from their growing presence in the urban economy and the regional political systems (see Upadhya 1988; Rutten 1995). They not only invest in the education of their children and aspire to be members of the urban middle classes; they also mobilize their caste, communities, and regional identities to consolidate their positions in the emerging economy.

Thus, the expansion of the middle class during the Nehruvian period also increased its fragmentation. This is also reflected in the nature of agitational politics during this period. Mobilizations for the redrawing of state boundaries on linguistic lines during the 1950s and 1960s, in the southern, northern, and western parts of India, were all led by the regional middle classes, belonging to specific upper/dominant caste communities. At some level these movements were aimed at renegotiating structures of power and dominance inherited from colonial rule. The newly emergent middle-class regional elite was no longer willing to work and survive under the political and economic domination of other linguistic/regional groups. They played a crucial role in articulating regional identities during this period. For example, the newly emergent middle-class Brahmins and Karans of the Orissa region (the present-day state of Odisha) mobilized the regional sentiment against domination by the Bengalis over the region. Similarly, Gujarat was carved out from Maharashtra in the 1960s when the dominant middle class of Maharashtra as well as that of Gujarat articulated a demand for two separate states. The middle-class leaders in the two different linguistic regions also came from specific castes communities. The story of Andhra Pradesh was also similar. In more recent times, new regional middle classes successfully articulated similar demands in Uttarakhand, Chhattisgarh, Jharkhand, and Telangana, leading to formation of new administrative units from the existing states of the Indian union. Interestingly, in almost all of these regions, those who led such regionalist movements emerged as the local political elite.

5

The Contemporary Dynamics and Number Games

They mostly live in rapidly growing cities and can afford cars, appliances and other conveniences that remain beyond the reach of most Indians. Theirs is the fastest growing demographic group in the country, and their buying power is expected to triple in the next 15 years, making India one of the most important consumer markets in the world.... (*New York Times*, 29 October 2011)

[If the middle income group] is to be reasonably secured in material terms, then India's ... [middle income group] constitutes less than 100 million people, and is crowded in the top decile along with the much smaller number of rich households. In that sense, India does not yet look much like the middle class societies of Latin America, let alone of the mature western democracies. (Meyer and Birdsall 2012: 9)

The decade of the 1980s is often viewed as an important turning point in the history of contemporary India. It was during the 1980s that the Nehruvian paradigm of development, which had hitherto been the dominant mode of thinking about changing the social and economic structure of Indian society, began to lose its sheen. The processes that produced this decline came from below, from above, and also from the side. The rise of a variety of 'new' social movements and the growing popularity of rights-based politics of marginalized groups questioned the value of such a model from 'below'. They pointed to the sufferings that the developmental process brought to a variety of communities and categories located on the margins of Indian society.

Even though the Nehruvian model of planning for development professed growth with equity and it indeed instituted programmes and policies for the inclusion of the marginalized in the process of development, it also further alienated and excluded many whose voices were not easily heard in the corridors of power. For example, it was often marginalized tribal communities who were displaced for the setting-up of large projects. Such groups and communities had to lose their sources of livelihood in the name of development. The rise of identity-based social movements among women, Dalits, and smaller ethnic communities also highlighted the blindness of such models of development to their distinctive cultures, aspirations, needs, and patterns of exclusions.

Some of this pressure from below was also a direct consequence of the positive change produced by the Nehruvian model of development. The first four decades of development planning and gradual institutionalization of democratic political institutions had succeeded in spreading a new culture of citizenship. This translated on the ground into ever increasing aspirations for inclusion of the historically deprived social categories. They began to assert their autonomy in the electoral and social domains and contested the developmental process that they perceived to be working against them. In other words, during the decade of the 1980s, the castes and communities located on the margins of Indian society, Dalits and lower sections of the officially defined Other Backward Classes (OBCs), began to move away from the politics of patronage and cosmetic inclusion within the dominant national parties and by the early 1990s, the political processes in India were shifting out of the vertical alliances to newer forms of horizontal mobilization around identities of caste and community, also described by some political scientists as a new democratic upsurge (Yadav 2000; Varshney 2000: 12). The women's movements raised hitherto unfamiliar and often uncomfortable questions about sexuality, culture, and power. The new social movements of the historically deprived social groups during the 1980s and 1990s were often outside the domain of electoral politics, articulated and led by the emerging middle classes in the language of 'rights' and also by invoking communitarian identities (see Jodhka 2001).

The Nehruvian paradigm of development planning was also questioned from above, by the emerging new thinking on economic growth, which aggressively advocated for a shift in the policy paradigm and successfully argued for the opening-up of Indian economy through neo-liberal reforms. The process of globalization that ensued soon after, during the early 1990s, was a manifestation of this process. It offered newer opportunities of economic growth, provided that India was willing to change its policy regime and participate in the promising economic opportunities. The business and corporate houses, India's private capital, that advocated some kind of state protection and support for its own development during the initial years after Independence, had acquired a sense of confidence by this time and wanted to be 'liberated' from the bureaucratic hurdles of the 'license and quota raj'.

The pressure to change also came from the 'side'. The collapse of the Soviet Union-led 'Eastern Bloc' in the global economy, the oil crisis due to wars in the Gulf region, and the challenges of managing foreign exchange in a fast changing global economy left very little space for the Indian state to carry on with old policies and perspectives on subjects like international trade, foreign capital, and currency regimes. The rapid spread of new telecommunication technology was revolutionizing the world, unleashing a new process of globalization, which appeared like a challenge but also offered many new opportunities for social and economic integration with the larger world.

Among those who enthusiastically welcomed the 'new' economic policy that began to unfold during the early years of the 1990s—liberalization, privatization, and globalization—were the Indian middle classes. Thus began a new chapter in the contemporary history of India. Not only did the middle class benefit economically from these reforms, the much higher growth that the Indian economy experienced during the post1990 period also expanded the middle class both horizontally as well as vertically. Horizontally speaking, its numbers grew very rapidly. It also experienced a vertical expansion as it further grew in diversity and newer sections from the rural hinterlands and margins increasingly identified themselves as middle class. Its influence over Indian society also grew. It soon became the norm, the way to be, for a variety of Indians. By the turn of the century almost everyone wanted to be a part of the middle-class story.

Even though the economic philosophy of the so-called neo-liberal policy regime was quite different from earlier development thinking, the Nehruvian phase of development had contributed quite positively in preparing and enabling India's economy for this new phase. As discussed in the previous chapters, the first three or four decades of state-mobilized investments in the core or 'basic' industries, and the import substitution policies that provided protection to private capital from outside competition, helped it acquire strength and confidence to collaborate with foreign capital and participate in the emerging global regime.

By default, the emerging global economic regime also created new space for educated and technically skilled Indians. The technically skilled with degrees from IITs, IIMs, and a large number of engineering colleges became readily available human resource for the rapidly expanding computer software sector and management of the new corporate industries, in India and in the expanding 'new economy' the world over.

This presents a complex and complicated scenario for a discussion on the Indian middle class. The middle class has been a major beneficiary of market-led growth processes. However, it is also the primary agency that articulates aspirations of identities—castes, communities, or regions—and speaks for them. To argue differently, the Indian middle class is placed quite centrally in this emerging scenario and it carries the burden of the balancing role in the 'new India'.

The Macro Context

Despite a rather lazy start, the Indian economy began to grow on a variety of fronts after the country gained independence from colonial rule. Even though the primary site of middle-class expansion during the first three or four decades was within the state system, the growth in the public sector and the administrative systems had implications for larger economic processes and created grounds for growth of private capital, which begins to be evident from the 1980s. As can be seen in Table 5.1, the growth rates of the Indian economy increased significantly during the 1980s, from an average of around 3 to 4 per cent until the early 1970s to nearly 8 per cent during the first decade of the 21st century.

This growth of the Indian economy was not simply quantitative but also qualitative. Even though demographically India continues to remain a predominantly rural society, with nearly two-thirds of its total population still living in rural areas, its economic structure has changed quite rapidly. At the time of India's independence, more than half of the national income came

TABLE 5.1 Plan-wise Growth Rates of the Indian Economy

Plan Period	Growth Rate (%)
First Plan, 1951–5	3.6
Second Plan, 1956–60	4.2
Third Plan, 1960–5	2.8
Fourth Plan, 1969–73	3.9
Fifth Plan, 1974–8	4.7
Sixth Plan, 1980–4	5.5
Seventh Plan, 1985–9	5.6
Eighth Plan, 1992–6	6.5
Ninth Plan, 1997–2001	5.5
Tenth Plan, 2002–6	7.7
Eleventh Plan, 2007–12	8.0

Source: Five Year Plan Documents (Eleventh and Twelfth Plans),
Planning Commission, Government of India.

from its primary sector, agriculture and allied activities.
By the 1990s, agriculture's contribution had come
down to nearly a quarter. The pace of this decline has
been much more rapid during the recent past. As is
evident from Table 5.2, the share of the primary sector
declined rapidly from 23.2 per cent in 1999–2000 to
less than 14 per cent in a little more than a decade
(2012–13). Even though manufacturing has not generated too many new jobs, India's tertiary or service
sector has been growing quite steadily (See Table 5.2).

TABLE 5.2 Changing Structure of the Indian Economy in Recent Years

Sector	1999–2000	2007–8	2012–13
Primary/Agriculture	23.2	16.8	13.9
Secondary/Industry	26.8	28.7	27.3
Tertiary/Services	50.0	54.4	58.8

Source: *Economic Survey, 2013–14*, Ministry of Finance, Government of India.

The rapid change evident from these numbers also shows the stark contradictions and challenges the Indian economy is confronted with. The increasing share of the service sector in the national economy clearly indicates the expanding economic value of its service economy, which in turn indicates the growing prosperity of the middle classes. However, the rapid decline of agriculture as a sector in terms of its contribution to the national income when nearly half of working Indians remain primarily employed in this sector implies the declining worth of its rural populace. Unlike many other parts of the world, where the rise of the middle class implied a decline of inequality, in India the pattern seems to be virtually opposite, a point we discuss in the following chapter.

The Emerging 'New' Middle Class(es)

The growing influence of the Indian middle class, particularly during the post-1990 period, has been talked about through two different yet overlapping perspectives. The first and the more popular one has been a simple income-centric or statistical view of the middle class. The second is a more substantive, qualitative or sociological view of the middle class. The first, income-centric view has been popularized by economists, financial institutions/consultants, and investment bankers who understand this social group in terms of an income threshold. Anybody earning an income equivalent to or more than the specified threshold qualifies to be in the middle class. They focus on income because of their interest in assessing the number or proportion of Indians who can actively participate in the market economy as consumers and sustain the market-led capitalist growth. This discourse has been particularly influential during the current period of the Indian middle class.

Their active participation in the market economy as consumers has indeed been an important attribute of the middle classes and discussion about them is abound everywhere in the contemporary world. However, the middle classes have also been an important historical category and a bearer of new values and lifestyles. Their engagement with the state as active members of the modern civil society has been critical in sustaining and promoting democratic regimes. They have been the source of creative energy in modern India and the world over. Thus, by implication, income levels, though critical, is only a qualifying criterion. Anyone who belongs to the middle-income category may not necessarily be a middle-class person, subjectively or on the basis of an objective sociological criterion. However, income levels could provide us with an easy starting point for a discussion on the contemporary situation of the Indian middle classes.

The Number Games

As is mentioned above, the economic turn during the 1990s quite fundamentally changed the orientation of the Indian economy. Neo-liberal reforms significantly raised the rates of economic growth, taking India out of what was pejoratively described by some economists as the 'Hindu rate of growth'. Not only did India open its economy to global capital and enthusiastically invite direct foreign investment, its economic contribution to the global economy also grew consistently.

Given that the Indian middle classes are popularly viewed as critical actors and agents in the emerging 'India story' in the global economy, estimating their numbers and future trends of growth has virtually became an obsession with a variety of institutions and actors in the academia and financial world. Mostly using available data sets on consumption patterns and asset ownership of Indian households, they have evolved definitions, methods of identifying middle-class individuals or households, and statistical cut off points that offer tentative estimates of the size of the Indian middle class.

The following table gives a brief overview of some of these efforts:

TABLE 5.3 Definitions and Estimations of the Size of the Indian Middle Class

Author(s)/Agency and Stated Objective	Definition of Middle Class	Estimation
Authors: Abhijit Banerjee and Esther Duflo (2008)	Households whose daily per capita expenditure valued at purchasing power	Does not estimate

Objective: To describe consumption choices, health and education investments, employment patterns, and other features of economic lives.	parity (PPP) is between USD 2 and 4 and those where it is between USD 6 and 10 (page 3). Basis: Living Standard Measurement Surveys	
Authors/Agency: NCAER, authored by Rajesh Shukla and Roopa Purusothaman (2008) Objective: To capture the rise in consumer spending to understand and project the expanse of markets in the coming years.	Households with an income of INR 250,000–1,250,000 at 2004–5 prices. Basis: Market Information Survey of Households, conducted by NCAER	Roughly 28 million households in 2009–10, approximately 15 per cent of the total Indian population
Authors/Agency: *The Mckinsey Quarterly*, authored by Eric D. Beinhocker, Dianna Farrell, and Adil S. Zainulbhai (2007) Objective: To understand consumer spending.	Households with a disposable income of INR 200,000 to 1,000,000 a year in real 2000 terms. Basis: Market Information Survey of Households, conducted by NCAER	50 million (roughly 5 per cent of the population)

(Contd.)

(*Contd.*)

Author(s)/Agency and Stated Objective	Definition of Middle Class	Estimation
Author: Nancy Birdsall Meyer Christian (2012) Objective: To estimate the size of the Indian middle class.	Minimum threshold of USD 10 per capita per day and a maximum threshold of USD 50 a day (2005 PPP).	69.17 million (roughly 6 per cent of the population)
	Minimum threshold of USD 8 per capita per day and a maximum threshold of USD 50 a day (2005 PPP).	91.4 million (roughly 7.75 per cent of the population)
	Basis: 66th Round NSS survey (2010)	
Author: Sudeshna Maitra (2007) Objective: To ascertain the size and consumption habits of the Indian middle class.	Households possessing a total of 12 durable items, 5 recreational goods (for example, tape players), 4 household goods (for example, refrigerators) and 3 transport goods (that is, cars) at the time of interview.	Lower-, middle-, and upper-class households constitute 20 per cent, 62 per cent and 18 per cent of urban households, respectively;
	55th Round of the Indian NSS survey (1999–2000)	this means 17 per cent of the entire Indian population

Authors/Agency: Deutsche Bank Research, authored by Steffen Dyck et. al (2009) Objective: To understand Asia's emerging middle class and its role in the expansion of the economy and political stability.	Households that own 70 per cent to 150 per cent of the household median net income of their respective countries	Does not estimate
Authors: Ernst and Young (undated) Objective: To examine the growth of the middle class in the emerging markets and explore how this will change both the developing and the developed worlds.	People earning between USD 10 and 100 per day. People in this income bracket can be considered a 'global middle class'—middle class by the standards of any country.	50 million people, or 5 per cent of India's population; the report projects that this group will grow steadily over the next decade, reaching 200 million by 2020
Agency: Asian Development Bank (2010)	Middle class as those with consumption expenditures of USD 2–20 per person per day in 2005 PPP.	Lower-middle class: 20.45 per cent Middle-middle class: 4.15 per cent

(*Contd.*)

(Contd.)

Author(s)/Agency and Stated Objective	Definition of Middle Class	Estimation
Objective: To estimate the size of the middle class across the developing Asian countries.	Lower-middle class—consuming USD 2–4 per person per day. Middle-middle class—between USD 4–10, is living above subsistence, and able to save and consume non-essential goods. Upper-middle class consumes USD 10–20 per day. Basis: World Bank's Povcal Net database	Upper-middle class: 0.5 per cent Total: 25.05 per cent
Author: Sonalde Desai (2001) Objective: To examine changes in the size and composition of the households falling in the upper tail of the consumption distribution.	Lower-middle class—households with per capita expenditure exceeding twice the poverty line but below four times the poverty line for the year. Upper-middle class—households with per capita expenditure exceeding four times the poverty line.	Lower-middle class: Of the total population, 11.21 per cent in 1983; 13.17 per cent in 1987–8; and 16.48 in 1993–4 Upper-Middle Class: Of the total population, 2.4 per cent in

	Basis: Various rounds of NSS survey	1983; 3.08 per cent in 1987–8; and 3.33 per cent in 1993–4
Author: Martin Ravallion (2009) Objective: To estimate the size of the middle-class population in the developing world.	Household with consumption per capita between USD 2 and 13 a day at 2005 PPP. The lower bound is the median poverty line of developing countries while the upper bound is based on the US poverty line.	146.8 million in the year 1990 (17.3 per cent of the total population) and 263.7 million (24.1 per cent of the total population) in the year 2005

These are a small but representative proportion of a large number of such estimations of the category. They all attempt to estimate the size of the Indian middle class and tend to converge around some common points. They all assume that the middle-income category has a critical role in India's development and economic growth, translating in or through expansion of the market and consumers. This is also a paradigm shift in the imagining of the Indian middle class, from Nehruvian development agents to the drivers of private consumption. Development effects of the rising numbers of middle-class Indians begin to be viewed differently, as an indication of a population moving out of poverty and into a class of consumers. Being middle class is to have sufficient amount of money to spend not only on eating and drinking but also on entertainment, education, health care, domestic infrastructure (Banerjee and Duflo 2008), leisure and travel, transport and communication, personal products, apparels, and so on (Kerschner and Huq 2011). By boosting demand for consumer goods, expansion of private consumption is by itself seen as a 'significant driver' of growth. The proportion of consumption expenditure in India was 57 per cent of the total GDP in 2008 and is close to that of developed nations such as Japan (55 per cent) and the US (71 per cent) (Kerschner and Huq 2011)

Economic Locations of the Indian Middle Class

Who are India's middle classes? Where are they located in the larger economic structure of the country? How is their location undergoing change with changes in the Indian economy?

Until the 1980s much of the middle class grew within the state-supported sectors. During the post-reform period, it grew with the expanding private sector of the Indian economy. However, this does not mean a switchover from 'public' to 'private'. Employment in public sector remains significant, much larger than the total employment in the organized private sector even 20 years after the initiation of economic liberalization. Table 5.4 provides estimations of employment strength in the organized sector of the economy from 1970–1 to 2010–11. This is precisely the sector where the middle class has always had maximum presence in the decades after Independence. Employment in the public sector grew from 11.2 million in 1970–1 to 19.14 million in 2000–1.

However, the state's policy on public employment can be disaggregated into two phases. The first is the period of expansion. Between 1970–1 to 1980–1 and 1980–1 to 1990–1, around 4.38 million and 3.58 million workers respectively were added to public sector employment. The 'thinning down of the state' discourse officially initiated in 1991 translated into a brake on the state's recruitment effort. During the next decade, between 1990–1 and 2000–1, merely 80,000 workers were added to the state's personnel strength. However, the attempt to thin down the state was most visible in the first decade of the 21st century when there appears to have been a moratorium on new recruitments while retirements continued. The total employment in the public sector saw a decline of as many as 1.59 million workers.

This is interesting because even though employment declined in the state sector, the Indian state did not experience any kind of 'shrinking'. Nor did development activities see any decline during this period. On the contrary, developmental and non-developmental expenditure of the central and the state governments rose by many folds, from INR 231.94 and INR 226.64 billion in 1980–1 to as much as INR 15,152.25 and INR 16,322.92 billion in 2012–13 respectively (RBI 2013).

Against the backdrop of such a mammoth increase in state expenditure, the reduction of jobs in the public sector could be attributed to a variety of rationalizations and structural adjustment policies advocating thinning down of the state. Even though the neo-liberal policies advocated a 'leaner state', in effect it only meant increasing instances of out-sourcing of official activities to private service providers and a kind of 'informalization' within the state system (GOI 2009).

TABLE 5.4 Employment in the Public and Organized Private Sectors (in millions)

Year	Public Sector (End-March)	Private Sector (End-March)
1970–1	11.10	6.73
1980–1	15.48	7.40
1990–1	19.06	7.68
2000–1	19.14	8.65
2010–11	17.55	11.45

Source: Table Collated from the *Handbook of Statistics on the Indian Economy: 2012–13*, p. 53, published by the Reserve Bank of India.

The state agencies began to contract out a number of developmental functions—electricity, sanitation, security, water supply, and so on—to private agencies with an inbuilt design of monitoring through user groups. This indeed has had far-reaching implications for the reproduction of the middle class through the Indian state and the politics of their relationship with the state.

Private Sector Employment

More importantly perhaps, the trend towards privatization and outsourcing of state services or the wider process of promoting economic activity through the private sector did not lead to a significant increase in organized private employment. Even though employment in organized private sector jobs grew from 6.73 million jobs in 1970–1 to 11.45 million jobs in 2010–11, the rate of its expansion was quite modest, only around 1 per cent per annum. Despite a significant expansion of the private sector in the Indian economy, its employment practices remain largely informal. According to *The Indian Labour and Employment Report* (ILER 2013), the Indian economy is overwhelmingly constituted by the unorganized sector. Nearly 84 per cent of the workforce in the Indian economy was employed in an unorganized and informal mode during 2011–12. Just about one-sixth of the total workers worked in the organized sector. Further, not everyone who is employed in the organized sector has social security benefits or permanency of job. Such workers make for more than half (60 per cent) of the 18 per cent employed in regular wage employment. Only a meagre 6.8 per cent of the total working Indians have regular jobs with all the statutory benefits. This is much smaller when we compare India with developed countries where regular employment could be above 50 per cent. In some countries, it even goes up to 80 per cent.

However, the so-called unorganized or informal sector is not a homogenous category. It has enormous diversity and internal differentiation. Not everyone working informally is poor or insecure. Even though a large proportion of those working in this sector are small-time self-employed, small and marginal farmers, petty-shop keepers, and low-wage earning workers in a variety of activities, the sector also includes those earning very high incomes, such as doctors, lawyers, chartered accountants, big farmers, and big shop-keepers. Besides the diversity of income and status, the unorganized sector is also differentiated by caste, religion, gender, and other similar social locations (Harriss-White 2003; GOI 2009).

This would also imply that a good proportion of the Indian middle class is also located in this sector. In purely economic terms, the middle-income groups would be located in all sectors of the economy—primary, secondary, tertiary, quaternary or the intel-lectual activities, and the quinary, the highest levels of decision making in a society or economy. As one would expect, a significant proportion of the middle classes are formally employed in the public and private sectors. However, statistically speaking, a larger proportion of them would be located in the private unorganized sector.

The *Economic Survey* of the central government (2014) notes that the compound annual growth rate (CAGR) of the service sector GDP at 8.5 per cent for the period 2000–1 to 2013–14 has been higher than the 7.1 per cent CAGR of overall GDP during the same period (GOI-MOF 2013–14). During the post-liberalization period, particularly during the first decade of the 21st century, the share of the service sector in the GDP has been increasing rapidly while that of agriculture has been steadily declining. The share of industry has remained more or less stagnant (also see Table 5.2).

Even though this rather rapid change in the structure of income in the Indian economy also reflects in the patterns of employment, the pace of change in the latter is much slower. As is evident from Table 5.5, even though the contribution of the primary sector to the national income is less than 14 per cent, it still provides employment to nearly half (48.9 per cent) of working Indians. However, a majority of working Indians are now employed outside the primary sector, in the service or tertiary sector and industry or the secondary sector. More importantly perhaps, the share of agriculture or the primary sector as a source of employment is steadily declining. This decline was quite significant during 1999–2000 and 2012–13: nearly 11 percentage points in a decade. Even though nearly 49 per cent of the working Indians are still reported as being employed in agricultural sector, a large majority of them also have subsidiary jobs, though mostly of informal nature.

TABLE 5.5 Share of Major Sectors in Total Employment (per cent)

Sector	1999–2000	2007–8	2012–13
Agriculture and Allied Activities	59.9	58.5	48.9
Industry	16.4	18.2	24.3
Services	23.7	23.3	26.9

Source: *Economic Survey*, Government of India 2013–14.

What are the broad conclusions? First, the primary sector of the Indian economy continues to be a source of main employment for nearly 49 per cent of working Indians even when its contribution to the total

GDP is less than 14 per cent; second, the service sector contributes more than 50 per cent to the GDP and its share has grown by almost 9 percentage points during the first decade of the current century. The service sector also employs more than a quarter of working Indians and this is likely to go up further. Given its pace of growth in terms of its share in national income and employment, a majority of those in the middle-income groups are likely to find their earning opportunities in the service sector. The manufacturing sector of the Indian economy also employs a quarter of working Indians and contributes the same proportion to the national GDP. This sector certainly has a lot of potential to grow and is also likely to offer employment opportunities at various levels, including for the middle classes.

Though agriculture continues to employ the largest proportion of working Indians, a large majority of workers in this sector do not fall in the middle-income category. Their consumption and expenditure pattern, a proxy for income, is abysmally low (ILER 2013). The middle-income households in rural areas are typically constituted by a relatively small number of large farmers, small entrepreneurs/shopkeepers, and salaried government servants. The secondary sector (industry) draws its middle-income households largely from manufacturing, mining, electricity, basic goods, intermediate goods, and consumer goods. Given the sluggish growth rates of the agricultural and industrial sectors, the tertiary sector has become the repository of a significant proportion of the middle-income earners in India (ILER 2013: 252).

Social Composition of the Middle-Income Group

What kinds of social backgrounds do these middle-income households come from? Are there any differences in terms of their caste, community, or other social origin variables? What do the available large data sets say on this subject? Using the monthly per capita consumption expenditure (MPCE) data available from the National Sample Survey Office (NSSO) as a possible proxy for income we can identify some patterns as presented in Table 5.6. This is based on the available data for 1999–2000 and 2011–12.

We could possibly divide the entire population into five consumption quintiles. The bottom MPCE quintile and the next 20 per cent can be taken as a proxy for poor and vulnerable households respectively. The next two MPCE quintiles can be taken as proxies for lower-middle-income and middle-income households respectively and the households in the last MPCE quintile can be considered as upper-middle income and rich households. A cross tabulation of the MPCE quintiles with social groups could provide us with a broad view of the presence of different social groups in each MPCE quintile. The social group classification is self-explanatory save 'Others', which is largely constituted by upper castes, mostly Hindus and Sikhs. A few others, such as the Jains, Parsees, and non-OBC Christians and Muslims, are also part of this group but their presence in the sample is likely to be nearly insignificant in statistical terms.

One will perhaps not be surprised to find a majority of the rural STs and SCs in the 'poor' and 'vulnerable' categories. This is true both for the data for 1999–2000 and for 2011–12. As many as 59 per cent of STs were in these two categories during 1999–2000 and despite India's high growth rates in the following decade, this proportion remains the same during 2011–12. Those clubbed with the official category of SCs, however, do experience some mobility during this period and move upwards. The proportion of SCs in the 'poor' and 'vulnerable' categories comes down from 52 per cent to 48 per cent during the same decade. In comparison to this, the share of 'poor' and 'vulnerable' in the so-called general category, who would largely be from the upper castes, remains at around a quarter of their population at both points of time. The OBCs occupy positions in the middle, with around 40 and 38 per cent of their total population being 'poor' and 'vulnerable' at both points of time under consideration. As one would expect, when we look at the proportions of each group in the middle and upper-middle income or rich categories, the statistical picture is completely reversed.

However, despite this persistence of correlation between caste and deprivation, the so-called middle-income groups are not socially homogenous. Even when the share of SC and ST communities is predictably lower among them, they are not entirely absent. Among the SCs, 17 and 18 per cent qualify to be in the middle-income category over the two periods of data collection. This figure is 14 and 15 per cent for the STs. Those listed as OBCs have a higher share in this category, above 20 per cent. But those from the upper castes or general category were above 30 per cent.

Patterns across social groups are not very different for urban India. Quite like rural settings, an overwhelming majority of the poor and vulnerable are from the SC, ST, and OBC communities. However, the proportion of SCs and OBCs among the poor and vulnerable is higher in urban India than is the case in rural areas. However, the urban STs are a little less likely to be poor or vulnerable than their counterparts living in rural areas. The share of poor general category is much lower, around 26 and 25 per cent at the two points of time, almost similar to their counterparts in rural areas. Likewise, when we look at the numbers for the middle and upper-middle income/rich categories, the statistical picture is again reversed.

Numbers Are Significant

Notwithstanding significant differences among those who have ventured to estimate the relative size of the Indian middle class in the total Indian population, they all seem to suggest that the Indian middle-class story is an important fact and its implications go beyond the local context. Even if they make for only 10 to 25 per cent of the total population of India, their absolute numbers are very large and would be larger than the most populous country of Europe. Even a small increase in its size in proportional terms would not only add a significant number to the potential buyers of consumer goods, it would also imply an improvement for those living below the line of poverty. The economists who look at the middle class from a growth perspective tend to agree that the expansion of the middle class is an important outcome and a useful evidence of economic growth (Meyer and Birdsall 2012; Ernst and Young [undated]; Ablett et al. 2007; Ravallion 2009).

However, the relationship of economic growth and middle-class expansion is not simply a one-way story. An expanding middle class has important politico-economic consequences. A large middle class tends be a source of political stability as it could help in build-ing consensus around the critical questions of eco-nomic policy (Easterly 2001). Similarly, an expanding middle class could be an enabling source for economic growth. Economists Abhijit Banerjee and Esther Duflo identify three distinct ways in which it could happen. First, the middle classes produce entrepreneurs who 'create employment and productivity growth for the rest of society'. Second, they could help in capitalist accumulation because they invariably emphasize on 'the accumulation of human capital and savings', thus enabling the economy to grow. Third, the middle class is a status and quality conscious social group and hence, they create demand for high quality goods. They normally have the capacity and are willing to pay extra, thereby encouraging firms to invest in production and marketing (Banerjee and Duflo 2008: 3; also see Lahiri 2014). The relationship of the middle class with economic growth is in a virtuous circle. Rising incomes translate into consumption, which further expands the market leading to economic growth, which in turn again results in even higher consumption, and economic growth. It is possible to find some evidence of this happening in contemporary India (Saxena 2010).

While numbers are indeed critical, the idea of the middle class is not exhausted by income classifications. As we have seen in earlier chapters, the middle class is an important sociological and historical category and an expansion in its size has implications beyond the economics of consumption. Social composition and political contexts also shape the middle class and are in turn shaped by such emergent social categories. This is discussed in the following chapters.

TABLE 5.6 Share of Population to Total Population of Each Social Group in Different Income Quintiles (in percentages)

MPCE Class	Rural							
	ST		SC		OBC		Others	
	1999–2000	2011–12	1999–2000	2011–12	1999–2000	2011–12	1999–2000	2011–12
Bottom 20 per cent (Poor)	37	36	27	25	19	18	10	11
Next 20 per cent (Vulnerable)	22	23	25	23	21	20	15	16
Next 20 per cent (Lower-Middle-Income Group)	17	17	20	20	21	21	20	20
Next 20 per cent (Middle-Income Group)	14	15	17	18	21	21	23	22
Top 20 per cent (Upper-Middle-Income Group and Rich)	10	9	11	13	18	20	32	31
Total	100	100	100	100	100	100	100	100

(*Contd.*)

| | Urban | | | | | | | |
| | ST | | SC | | OBC | | Others | |
MPCE Class	1999–2000	2011–12	1999–2000	2011–12	1999–2000	2011–12	1999–2000	2011–12
Bottom 20 per cent (Poor)	30	31	33	31	25	24	13	11
Next 20 per cent (Vulnerable)	23	20	26	24	24	23	16	15
Next 20 per cent (Lower-Middle-Income Group)	18	19	20	20	22	21	19	19
Next 20 per cent (Middle-Income Group)	16	16	14	16	17	18	24	23
Top 20 per cent (Upper-Middle-Income Group and Rich)	13	13	7	10	12	14	29	31
Total	100	100	100	100	100	100	100	100

Source: Various rounds of National Sample Survey.
Note: Figures are rounded off to the nearest zero.

6

Consuming Identities and Exclusionary Powers

Advertisements and media images have contributed to the creation of an image of a 'new' middle class, one that has left behind its dependence on austerity and state protection and has embraced an open India…. The newness of the middle class rests on its embrace of social practices of taste and commodity consumption…. Images of mobility associated with newly available commodities … serve to create a standard, which the urban middle classes can and should aspire to. In this process, the new (urban) Indian middle class becomes a central agent for the re-visioning of the Indian nation in the context of globalization. (Fernandes 2000: 89)

As is evident from the previous chapter, notwithstanding disagreements on its extent or pace, almost everyone estimating the number of middle-class Indians agrees that their size has been growing over the years and in most likelihood, it will continue to grow at a reasonably good pace in the coming decades. They also tend to agree that even when their proportions remain low in the total population of India, their absolute size is substantial. Even if middle-class India were to be a mere one-fifth or one-fourth of India's total population, it would perhaps be greater than the total population of the largest country of developed Western Europe.

Interestingly, this expansion is not confined to their numbers. The idea of the middle class, as a subjective category of self-identification, has also been expanding. A much larger proportion of people living in urban India, and increasing numbers living in rural settlements, are today likely to identify them as belonging to the middle class. In the urban context, such individuals could range from a 'low' level employee earning a few thousand rupees per month in the organized sector to a rich professional earning more than a million rupees every month from his or her private business. Even

141

those working part-time as cultivators and owning agricultural land prefer to be viewed as middle class, if they happen to be educated and simultaneously have an active relationship with urban or non-agricultural economic activity. This growing diversity and differentiation within the middle class also makes the category rather 'amorphous' and too general for a meaningful sociological analysis (Srivastava 2009; Fernandes 2006; Mankekar 1999; Dickey 2012).

At another level, this growing popularity of middle class as a category of self-identification among a wide variety of Indians is also an indicator of changing structural and cultural realities of contemporary Indian society where being middle class becomes more meaningful than the ascribed identities of caste, kinship, and ethnicity. Even when the identity of middle class is invoked as a hyphenated category, such as the Dalit middle class or the Muslim middle class, it inevitably points towards a process of increasing internal differentiation within these social/ethnic groups and categories.

How does one make sense of this shift in the imaginations and identities of selves in a variety of contexts? What exactly is gained or being conveyed through such a claim of being members of the middle class over a 'traditional' or a particularistic social identity among members of otherwise heterogeneous and internally diverse and differentiated social groups? What is distinctive about the contemporary context of middle class in India, the so-called neo-liberal times?

In order to understand this complex social phenomenon, we need to move away from the statistical view of middle class that identifies it purely on the basis of the amount of income a person or a household earns. An income-centric discourse merely captures anyone and everyone who can situate himself/herself in the market through his/her purchasing power at a certain arbitrarily set threshold as middle class. The approach therefore becomes blind to social composition and other cultural and political dynamics that occur within the broad social category of the middle class. In such a discourse, even spatial, occupational, and educational differences become insignificant except for underlining the fact that the proportion of the middle class is significantly more in urban than in rural areas. As we have discussed in the first chapter of this book, middle class is also a historical category and its social profile and political imagination changes with time.

The 'Neo-Liberal' Times and the Consuming Middle Class

As we have seen in the previous chapter, neo-liberal economic reforms initiated during the early 1990s changed the thrust and priorities of India's economic policy. While on one hand the shift in economic policy helped the Indian economy grow at an accelerated pace, at another level, the 'opening' up of Indian markets unleashed a new regime of consumption. Even though agricultural production and industrial manufacturing remained important, the new economic policy was oriented towards the potential consumer, who could sustain demand in the marketplace for a wide variety of consumer goods. The removal of restrictions on the import of consumer goods also implied that those Indians who had money in their pockets could now buy virtually everything in the local market, from fancy cars and computers to cosmetics and cameras.

An important aspect of the new consumer culture is also the growing ascendance of popular media and the new modes of seducing potential buyers through images projected on television screens and pages of newspapers and magazines. These images not only seduce a wide range of consumers with differing sizes of their pockets but also become critical for social life, electoral politics, and cultural identities. Media images begin to be viewed as normatives of a good and socially appropriate life-style. More than anything else, the 'media revolution' of the 1990s begins to influence and shape middle-class identities and their notions of self-realization and freedom.

In the emerging context of the increasingly mediated social and cultural life, consumption becomes the new idiom of mobility, achievement, and identity. Leela Fernandes rightly argues that the discourse or debate on this new middle class is centred on its 'culture of consumption' that has expanded with new commodities becoming available in the Indian market after the shift in economic policy during the early 1990s, 'liberalization'. Fernandes is not the only one to point this out. Other writings on the contemporary Indian middle class also similarly argue that consumption has come to be a critical arena for the reproduction of middle-class identity in South Asia today (Appadurai and Breckenridge 2005; Oza 2006, Liechty 2003). The implication of this focus on consumption is obviously that it gives primacy to the amount of disposable income a person has in his/her pocket. However, consumption is not simply an economic activity. It also implies a 'style of life', a culture that reproduces itself through a continuous, almost obsessive, involvement with commodities and their consumption. Thus, this 'new' or post-liberalization Indian of middle class is very different in terms of its values and attitudes from the 'old' middle class, which, as Nita Mathur rightly argues:

> … distinguished itself from the elite and commoners or the general public… in terms of its emphasis on the virtues of diligence, conscientiousness, individual achievement and commitment to the national interest. It articulated its distinction and respectability in society by critiquing the indisputably affluent lifestyle that characterised the *nawabs*, *taluqdars* and aristocratic elites…. The Indian middle class established certain benchmarks for social and moral order…. (Mathur 2010: 215)

In contrast, for the 'new' Indian middle class, the primary concern is largely 'self-making' through acquisition of a lifestyle, primarily associated with possession of status goods. Comparative instincts and competitive processes in which individuals try and keep up with the norms of the social group with which they seek to identify also govern consumption as a social activity. This indeed has a larger normative and sociological dimension, which shapes political imagination. Consumption becomes a modality of social life (Appadurai and Breckenridge 1995).

Economic liberalization in India has been synonymous with globalization and this is clearly reflected in new identities of middle-class Indians, 'in both cultural and economic terms; in cultural terms by defining a new cultural standard that rests on the socio-symbolic practices of commodity consumption and in economic terms as the beneficiaries of the material benefits of jobs' in the 'new economy' (Fernandes 2000: 88). This expansion or globalization of the Indian economy also translates on the ground into new aspirations and identities. For example, professionals belonging to information and technology sector in Chennai proudly told Fuller and Narasimhan (2007) about the distinctive value of their newly acquired economic status while being interviewed for a study. 'The money meant that they could now enjoy very comfortable standards of living comparable with that *available in the west*'

(Fuller and Narasimhan 2006: 134, emphasis added). A young man working in a multi-national company in Delhi gave an almost ditto answer to another sociologist, Nita Mathur, while counting his achievements over a short period of time in service of the company:

> MNCs provide attractive salaries to starters and people like me with only two years of work experience; those who work in an MNC get better exposure and opportunities to travel from one country to another and to adopt a cosmopolitan lifestyle. (Mathur 2010: 218)

At another level, the neo-liberal rise of a middle-class normative in urban India also means ascendance of money as the most critical signifier of status, sometimes transcending (or working together with) other identities such as caste, community, or gender. 'Money is the most important thing in Madurai, even more than *jāti*';[1] 'if a person is well off, people will look at him

---

[1] Indian social structure is divided into four *varna*s (it eventually grew into five). The closest English translation of 'varna' will be caste. Caste is a social grouping of the population into mutually exclusive, hereditary, endogamous, and occupation-specific *varna*s. There are four *varna*s: Brahmins (priests), Kshatriyas (warriors), Vaisyas (traders), and the

respectfully, no matter what his jāti is' (Dickey 2012: 225), were some of the predictable responses when anthropologist Sara Dickey interviewed her relatively less privileged respondents in the south Indian town.

Consumption in Madurai was not simply about eating well and living comfortably. It made the individual get 'counted in society', be 'visible', and acquire 'dignity' (Dickey 2012: 226). 'Consumption was deployed to negotiate middle-class recognisability' by those who wished to identify themselves as such. Their recognition in society as members of the middle class depended on some 'critical consumption practices', their ability to buy and demonstrate the possession of those commodities (Dickey 2012: 221).

Sudras (menial workers) and the Ati Sudras (the untouchables, doing the lowest category of the menial jobs). As the population rose and economy became more complex, the *varna* system evolved into *jati*s (closest English translation will again be caste). Although *jati*s share the same characteristics of *varna*, there are considerable regional variations in the evolution of *jati*s. The same *jati* can be classified backward in one region but excluded from the list of backwards in another.

Being middle class and elite is more than just being rich. 'Critical consumption practices' also have to be acquired and cultivated, such as bird watching tourism, or the ability to appreciate art and other forms of recreation/entertainment that resemble cosmopolitan cultural forms. All these become consuming lifestyle features of contemporary middle classes (Urfi 2012; Kochhar 2004: 20). The shift also has a larger meaning for the country. Consumption, as Upadhya argues, is now seen as a substitute for development and the middle class as its flag bearer (Upadhya 2008).

Those who produce consumer goods make sustained attempts to seduce increasing numbers of people into the public culture of consumption through fierce advertisement campaigns, electronic and print media/ channels, films, sports, shopping malls, promotion of tourism, hotels, restaurants, clubs, and so on. Even visiting a hospital for routine medical examination and clinical tests is often less of a medical requirement than an act of seeking social status by going to fancy corporate/private hospitals which look like five star hotels. As Lefebvre argues, corporate hospitals actively advertise and position themselves as part of a consumerist vision of healthcare (Lefebvre 2008).

Identity seeking through consumption weakens social differences and telescopes the middle classes towards a single destination (Jaffrelot and van der Veer 2008:12). It also reflects a certain kind of empowerment of the individual who can consume the ever-increasing supply of goods and services. Unlike the traditional status hierarchies of caste and kinship, middle-class statuses are, in principle, open and individually achievable. As a part of the growing basket of consumable services, an increasing number of customized paid courses/services offered by specialized agencies to develop personality traits have become available in a range of urban centres in India (see Srivastava 2014).

Such subjects used to be earlier discussed with close friends and relatives behind closed doors or in the confession box of a church. Bold advertisements persuading individuals to consult for personality development like courage, self-confidence, peace of mind, freedom from resentment and regret, ability to fully express your love, ability to make decisions without doubting oneself, different ways of achieving happiness in private lives now routinely appear on television screens and on social media. They are all matters of consumption. Among other services on offer to the contemporary middle class are education at different levels, health clubs, spiritual discourses, personalized sexual therapies and consultations, customized Ayurveda treatments, yoga sessions, dancing classes, Formula One racing, membership of golf courses and clubs, museum visits, art, paintings, photography expeditions, wine tasting, adventurous and water sports, foreign language lessons, visits to theme parks, and many more (see Brosius 2010). Being beautiful and healthy also becomes a part of the consumption culture that could be acquired through visiting parlours and health clinics, provided one has enough money in one's pocket.

Gender Effects

This consumption-centric culture around which the contemporary middle class constructs its identities has important implications for gender identities. Media-centric culture has begun to influence and shape notions of individual freedom and empowerment.

As mentioned above, the question of gender equality and women's rights has been a part of the mainstream political discourse, a promise made by the independent Indian state to its women. However, patriarchal social structure and mental dispositions are hard to change. Constitutional promises and rigid structures on the ground often come into conflict. The expanding size of Indian middle classes, growing aspirations, and mobility has meant an increasing number of women going out to study and work. It was in this wider context that the decades of 1970s and 1980s witnessed influential mobilizations by urban middle-class women[2] against everyday street violence, traditional practices such as dowry, and for greater representation in the nation's political life. Over the years the gender question acquired a kind of mainstream status. Giving representation to women in different spheres of life has become a part and parcel of the 'politically correct' things to do.

The onset of economic reforms in the 1990s and the growing reach of neo-liberal economic philosophy through media images and shifts in political discourse also appropriated this feminist discourse by underlining the critical significance of individual self-realization,

---

[2] These mobilizations were not always confined to urban centres or to the middle classes and often involved women from rural areas bringing in their own concerns to the women's movements.

which could be achieved in the new dispensation through individual entrepreneurship and pleasure seeking consumption. As Chaudhuri argues, in the neo-liberal economy with market supremacy, 'women were free to both achieve and enjoy' (Chaudhuri 2014: 152). She sums up this connection between the new notion of women's empowerment and ascendance of the neo-liberal market economy quite well:

> [The] projection of 'unfettered' self ... was equally a projection of economic liberalization, the concerned social context that made this 'freedom' possible, ... unimaginable in the Nehruvian epoch of license raj and state control.... Celebration of this new-found 'self' of the Indian women was therefore a simultaneous celebration of India's economic reforms. (Chaudhuri 2014: 152)

However, the new media images also actively project Indian women as being Indian in a distinctive way. Unlike the modern market-driven Western culture, where the individual autonomy of its middle-class women has presumably been a reality for long, the Indian woman is almost always presented as being able to carry an element of tradition with her, even when she travels in the market-driven globalized world. This is true not only about the young woman who gets selected as the beauty queen, amongst the most beautiful women of the world in a given pageant, but also about the successful professional IT worker, medical doctor, or corporate head, whose media representations show her successfully and happily managing both her professional duties and the children and husband at home, and doing well on both the fronts.

This can neither be easy, nor real. However, this ideational notion of 'finding a balance', Smitha Radhakrishnan argues, makes the Indian experience of globalization gendered in a specific way. While it is viewed as 'progress', it also asks for a kind of 'sacrifice' from women who wish to be individually successful in their professional life. In her interviews with IT professional women in the city of Bangalore and in Silicon Valley in the US, Radhakrishnan found this narrative of finding a 'balance' between 'individual, family and community responsibilities' as a 'recurring theme' (Radhakrishnan 2008: 12).

However, at another level, this mainstreaming of the gender question and its advocacy through popular media also opens up new spaces for the middle-class woman that were not earlier available to her. Sex ratios in India have tended to worsen with social and economic mobility, with families choosing sex-selective abortions in favour of having male children. However, as the upwardly mobile stabilize in a middle-class location, parents tend to accept daughters more easily (see Kaur and Bhalla 2015) and aspire for their education and their careers as they do for their sons. A study by Ruchika Ganguly-Scrase among the lower-middle classes in Bengal shows this quite clearly:

> Parents frequently provide positive encouragement to girls to study so that a good education would better equip them to enter the work force. Such expectations were previously absent among lower-middle-class families. Nowadays, not only is women's education a source of pride for parents, it also stands as a safety net: an insurance against a daughter's failed marriage or widowhood. (Ganguly-Scrase 2003: 554)

Interestingly, even when Ganguly-Scrase tries to suggest that economic liberalization might shrink employment opportunities for women, her respondents often argued back with passion that opportunities for women had certainly become better in the recent past.

Beyond Consumption

Urbanization and expansion of middle class has indeed brought about a greater fluidity in social life, giving a larger number of choices to individuals. However, being in the middle class in India rarely means emancipation from prejudice or social and economic dependencies. The wide range and variety of consumable goods and services come for a range of prices depending upon their quality and 'class'. Thus, while at one level, consumption dissolves differences of status; at another level it produces a new set of status hierarchies. It is here that we need to recognize the obvious limits to the 'fluidity' brought about by consumption in the social sphere. While the new culture of consumption indeed offers possibilities of individual social and symbolic mobility, the older boundaries of caste and community do not disappear. Nor do the realities of economic inheritance and acquired social capital/social network become irrelevant. On the contrary, they tend to condition the emergent hierarchies, within the middle class and in its relation to those located below it. In other words, notwithstanding its 'modernity', membership of the middle class is constrained by pre-existing privileges and hierarchies. Despite its apparent claim to individualization, members of the contemporary middle classes often act collectively, preserve privileges, and construct boundaries that exclude (see Beteille 2013). As Kapur puts it, 'for a putative middle class to act as a class and articulate [and preserve] its interest, one must think beyond income and consumption as the defining trait of the middle class' (Kapur 2010: 158).

The Politics of the Contemporary Middle Class

The contemporary Indian middle class is as much constituted by its social history and by the politics of the day as by the economics of contemporary times. Over the past decades, it has emerged as a hegemonic class, a distinct privileged group, which has assets (land and other properties), capabilities (modern/English education), and invariably social/cultural capital (networks and status). This class has acquired the legitimacy to speak on behalf of the larger society (while articulating 'universal concerns') or for its specific community (while articulating 'particularistic concerns'). It is in the backdrop of this instrumental, yet socially rooted, definition of middle class that this section of the chapter tries to interrogate the mutual relationship between middle-class politics and culture and the state, economy, and the society in contemporary India.

The so-called old Indian middle class, though enjoying a hegemonic position, had a different kind of relationship within institutions of power. Through its critical location and social/cultural capital, it acquired a naturalized position of leadership with a considerable amount of authority over decisions about what is right or wrong for the country and its people. The characteristic features of middle-class ideology during this phase were a belief in the parliamentary form of democracy, secularism, respect for diversity, and support for welfare provisions and affirmative action to ameliorate the living conditions of the poor and the historically disadvantaged. It supported state initiatives in the economic sphere through direct investments in the public sector. As we have discussed earlier, this middle class saw itself as an important agency of the nation-building project. However, although the middle class claimed to represent national interest, the policy architecture, whether unconsciously or by design, largely created conditions which made this class the biggest beneficiary of the state's policies.

The contemporary or the 'new' middle class no longer appears to be championing the task of nation building or the state-led initiatives for economic growth. Nor does it actively support efforts for poverty alleviation or pro-active policies and programmes of the state for the disadvantaged. As Deshpande rightly argues,

> having consolidated its social, economic and political standing on the basis of the development state, this group is now ready to kick it away as the ladder it no longer needs. (Deshpande 2003: 150)

However, it does not mean that the Indian middle class has become completely globalized and it does not need or identify with the nation. On the contrary, as Deshpande puts it, its identification and claim over the nation has only become more hegemonic, albeit differently, from a position of 'proxy' to that of 'portrait'.

> ... the middle-class no longer claims merely to represent the people (who alone were thought to constitute

the nation in the era of development), but rather that
it is itself the nation. (Deshpande 2003: 150)

Having exhausted the historical potential of the
state to serve its interests and enable its expansion, the
Indian middle class turned to the market for its further
growth and consolidation; to meet its ever increasing
desire for higher earnings, material possessions, leisure,
and consumption. This also changed its ideology and
identity. Along with those in the corporate sector,
middle-class leaders now actively advocate market-
based instruments for managing and organizing the
economy and society. They see 'too much bureaucracy
and too little enterprise' in the Nehruvian developmental state and aggressively advocate the 'need to
reduce the role of the state and turn to the market as a
catalyst of development' (Kothari 1991: 555). The state
begins to be increasingly viewed as a site of corruption
and patronage while the market is seen as rewarding
merit and performance (Chatterjee 2011).

At another level, quite like its role in the earlier
phase, the 'new' Indian middle class provides the necessary legitimacy to policies of economic liberalization
and privatization initiated by the state during the 1990s

(Kohli 2008). As a class, its members had already accumulated the required skill and asset capability to enter the market and reap its benefits. The middle class thus made this transition from 'development' to 'globalization' rather 'smoothly' (Deshpande 2003: 150).

Inequalities and Exclusions

Interestingly, the trajectory of the Indian middle class's growth and its politics appears to be quite different from its counterparts in the Western world. Middle classes grew in Western countries during the 20th century to an extent that many of them effectively became middle-class societies with more than 90 per cent of the population identifying themselves as middle classes. This did not happen because of the growing reach of markets and consumer culture. On the contrary, this was largely a result of an active welfare state and gradual expansion of entitlements and extension of citizenship rights in the form of universal provision of health care, quality education and housing, and so on. Gosta Esping-Andersen describes this as a process of 'de-commodification', which 'occurs when a state's services are rendered as matter of right, and when a person can maintain livelihood without reliance on the market' (Esping-Andersen 1990: 22).

Individuals can transform their labour into commodity—goods, services, or ideas—only when they have assets of capabilities. Lack of skill and capabilities translates into a precarious and vulnerable existence. De-commodification requires a pro-active welfare regime and a corresponding institutional structure that can facilitate building of assets and capabilities of the citizens. This helps them integrate themselves with the market society. Gupta reminds us that the development of the middle class in the Western context was in fact a 'de-commodification' project. It was a project to bridge the gap between the privileged and the rest of the society. Such a project was actualized through the expansion of socio-economic welfare measures spearheaded by the state (Gupta 2009: 83) whereas the contemporary middle class in India is created through the market which produces exclusionary, rather than inclusionary effects.

The contemporary Indian middle class, which roughly makes for less than a quarter of its population (as per the most generous estimates), celebrates the market as the ultimate panacea for all the problems encountered by Indian society, its economy, and politics. Global economic experiences show that greater reliance on markets tends to shrink, rather than expand middle classes. It also increases disparity and inequalities, often producing marginalization for millions.

Instead of supporting or demanding welfare measures by the state, dominant sections of the Indian middle class are often critical of welfare schemes for the poor because they presumably take away the resources required for investment in capital goods and infrastructure. Lack of the latter is assumed to impact negatively on the prospects of economic growth. Thus, instead of levelling differences and inequalities, such a socio-political process reinforces older inequalities and produces newer ones. As Fernandes writes,

> ... the new middle-class does not just incorporate pre-existing forms of inequality, it also generates inequality. The classificatory practices through which individuals attempt to gain access to membership within the new middle class are about both access and restriction. The acquisition education, for instance, is the most evident strategy of upward mobility for a wide range of social groups.... New middle-class strategies simultaneously transform education into a thicker set of class practices

that are contingent on a wide range of socio-cultural distinctions based on language, lifestyle, credentials, residence—distinctions that encode historically produced inequalities such as those of caste and language. (Fernandes 2011: 76)

She goes on to argue that it is for this reason that the dominant or the 'hegemonic new middle class still largely comprises segments of the upper-caste Hindu middle-classes' (Fernandes 2011: 76). More often than not, it is they who have a functional grip over the English language and are able to capitalize on new employment opportunities, particularly in the private sector. The success of the upper echelons of the middle class is admired and sought to be emulated so much so that it has become, what she calls, a symbol of 'normative standard for the larger social group' (Fernandes 2011: 74).

Given that access to quality education is the most critical vehicle for upward mobility and for enhancing capability, the contemporary middle class forcefully opposes any policy design creating institutional frameworks and unfolding a level playing field through affirmative action policies. Merit becomes the desired criterion for acquiring the education valued by the markets. In practice, advocacy for merit is merely a self-preservation strategy achieved through monopoly over private education, entry into university, and class endogamy (Peace 1984).

The economic reforms of the 1980s and 1990s, globalization, and the rise of the new middle class in India have also been accompanied by the emergence of a new kind of politics which celebrates civil society organizations over political parties and trade unions. This shift disempowers the poor and lower castes since decision-making structures are taken out of political processes where the poor tend to have significant presence (Baviskar 2011) simply because of their larger numbers. This nature of middle-class activism eliminates institutional spaces available to the poor for articulating their demands or registering their protests.

Local level resident associations are a good example of such exclusionary politics. In her study of such organizations in Mumbai, Hélène Zérah (2007) found that through such activism, those living in middle-class localities came together and mobilized political support for the removal of hawkers. The emerging patterns in new urban settlements also reflect attempts of the Indian upper-middle class to insulate itself from the realities of urban life. This includes restructuring spatial patterns in cities, where an increasing number of the middle-class rich move to gated residential communities. In the context of the thinning of the state discourse and the consequent depletion of state funding for public amenities, municipalities are increasingly passing the burden of services which are supposed to be provided by them to resident associations. These associations are able to privately bear the cost of municipal services due to the collective economic capacity of their members.

As a consequence, some of the basic municipal services are withdrawn not only from gated communities but also from low income housing areas. Further, the cultural standards of 'clean', 'hygienic', and 'peaceful' living coaxes the residential association to attempt (mostly successfully) to remove encroachments and petty commercial establishments from in and around their gated colonies. The drive to clean and beautify cities and build infrastructure such as wide roads for the use of private vehicles sees urban poverty as a problem and hence the clamour to forcibly evacuate the 'illegal' occupant residing in slums and on the side of the roads. Thus, the gated colonies of the new middle class, which itself is a symbol of consumption, also become the means for institutionalizing disparity and for a variety of exclusionary social and political practices in the emerging urban India (Kundu 2011: 23–5; Kamath and Vijayabaskar 2009; Harriss 2007).

'Consumption' too has its exclusionary effects, as pointed out by many students of the contemporary Indian middle class. 'Existential reality of being a middle-class Indian is an inescapable desire to escape the rest of India,' argues Krishna Sankaran (2006: 2327). Similarly, Malcom Voyce sees the emerging shopping malls as exclusionary spaces, virtual monopolies of a certain class of people who consider themselves culturally superior and are able to afford the cost of consumption, for leisure, of food and expensive goods. They are 'social fortresses', which separate the middle-class consumers from those unwanted elements who are seen as being ineligible for a high quality life and incapable of participating in the new economics of governance. Forging a new middle-class identity, the malls help them to render invisible the needs of the working class and the poor (Voyce 2007).

7

Diversities and Margins

The [middle] class is not just one grey amorphous mass. It is instead a spectrum of many colours, an aggregate of many subcultures, each with its own shape and brilliance; its own traditions and aspirations; its own constraints and ambitions.[1]

As we have repeatedly argued in this book, middle class is not only an economic category, or simply a matter of being placed in an income-consumption bracket, but also a social identity. Its emergence and expansion has profound political implications for the larger political system. The idea and identity of the middle class has a historical context. Middle classes, as we understand

[1] Quoted in B.M. Bhatia 1994: 87.

them today, emerged and expanded in modern liberal democracies. A larger middle class is assumed to be good for democratic politics. It presumably helps in blunting the possible skirmishes that inequalities inevitably generate in market-based capitalist societies.

The consolidation of democratic regimes in countries of Western Europe during the 20th century accompanied an expansion of the middle class in those societies. Even though income inequalities persisted, the growing identification with middle-class identity brought about a sense of common-ness and homogeneity. It was not simply about increased income levels of the erstwhile poor and those from the working classes. Being and becoming middle class also changed life-styles and modes of social and political behaviour. As we have discussed earlier, this expansion of middle-class identity followed a degree of dissolution of the traditional hierarchies of status/rank and an advent of new notions of citizenship based on ideas of equality, fraternity, and fairness. Differences of ethnicity, race, or gender persisted. But the expansion of the middle class helped in evolving a democratic public sphere in which nearly everyone could participate as equal members of the national political community.

The Indian middle-class experience has been different. Socially, culturally, and geographically India is among the most diverse regions of the world today. Its social diversities are both horizontal as well vertical. Horizontally, India has diversities of religion, ethnicity, and language. Vertically it has diversities and hierarchies of caste, tribe, and race. Diverse cultures and communities are not only viewed as being different from each other but they are also judged or valued as being unequal. Even though the national identity has over the years and decades become stronger, some of the diversities have also become sharper. Hierarchies of caste and tribe have also persisted.

The middle class has been an important actor in the process of making and representing diversities. As we have seen in the previous chapters, the emergence of a middle class during the colonial period played an important role in producing a common national identity. It was through its activities that modern institutions and democratic culture were taken to different regions of the Subcontinent. It provided leadership to the nationalist movement and played an active role in the nation building process after Independence. However, members of the middle class have also played a key role in shaping and sustaining India's diversities. They have provided leadership to all kinds of identity movements, of regions, castes, and communities. Some of these identity based political movements had already emerged during the colonial period but they multiplied over the years and acquired prominence during the post-1980s in Indian politics. Besides providing leadership to a diversity of social groups and communities, members of the middle classes within these groups have also actively participated in the framing and articulation of social and cultural differences among the groups.

Middle Class and the Politics of Diversity

The idea of diversity is invoked in contemporary India in four interrelated ways. First and foremost, middle-class leaders representing diverse groups invoke the idea of diversity simply to describe the complexities of social, cultural, and economic realities that constitute contemporary India. They demand from the state system recognition of the pre-existing social and political pluralities, at the regional as well as national levels. This claim can take diverse forms, ranging from seeking representation in political and constitutional bodies; advocacy for recognition of their language: budgetary allocation for promotion of their communitarian art and culture: constructing memorials for their community icons; lobbying for declaring public holidays on the birth/death anniversary of their leaders: and so on. Second, they try to deploy the idea of diversity as a normative principle on which these realities should be valued, endorsed, and accommodated.

The logical conclusion of upholding these two principles is the acceptance and recognition of diversity not merely as a lip service but as a matter of right. At a broader level, it would also imply challenging the universalism embedded in the idea of the individual citizen embedded in notions of democracy, equality, and equal opportunity. Instead, they ask for a state system or a nation embedded in the principle of difference. This 'right to diversity' also challenges the presumed power of the majority, both sociologically as a rule of the 'dominant group' or identities, and normatively, as a notion of 'good' or 'fair' society. Thus, individual members of the middle class come to represent politics of diversity framed through a range of social identities—caste, religion, region/language, gender, or ethnicity.

At the operational and policy level, these identities are articulated in the discourse of representation, social justice, affirmative actions, and access to equal opportunity—broadly in the language of citizenship. However, the nature of these claims is often complex and not free of tensions and conflict. For example, even when they demand equal citizenship in the framework of modern democracy, assertion of difference also has the risk of slipping into nostalgia for the 'past tradition' and 'going back', often invoking the ideas of patriarchal and non-democratic modes of social life.

Some of these regional or identity-based claims and mobilizations have had far-reaching implications for the Indian political system. One good example of this is the emergence of various regional political parties during the 1970s and later. The logic of these regional parties was that the existing political formations did not reflect the plurality of social cleavages present in Indian society. In other words, national level political parties were not able to reflect regional needs and aspirations.

Even though these political processes reflect changing realities on the ground, often in rural and agrarian settings, middle-class individuals play an active role in articulating the agenda of these political parties. At the same time, in many cases, the rise of regional political parties was accompanied and galvanized by consolidation of a caste or caste-like identity. The rise of the Samajwadi Party in Uttar Pradesh, the Lok Jan Shakti Party in Bihar, and the National Lok Dal in Haryana are good examples of this process. In other cases, such politics could also present itself as a combination of language, caste, and regional aspirations. The Dravida Munnetra Kazhagam (DMK) and the All India Anna Dravida Munnetra Kazhagam (AIADMK) in Tamil Nadu, the Akali Dals in Punjab, and more recently the Trinamool Congress (TMC) in West Bengal represent this trend. At the political level, these regional identity based formations ask for devolution of political power and tend to invariably promote a caste/community/ language group-specific politics in their region.

However, the role of middle-class members in these political parties is quite complex. This complexity is reflected in their support for politics of diversity while selectively also abiding with the politics of the dominant middle class. In other words, there is vociferous support for politics of diversity based on the

175

articulation of a regional discourse, autonomy and devolution of political power, respect and national status to their language, political representation through regional or caste identity, respect and promotion of regional culture/aspirations; all of which should not get subsumed under the attempt of homogenization, almost inevitably promoted by all nation-states.

Even when they articulate a regional agenda, in most cases members of the middle class do not reject the idea of a democratic nation-state. They complain about the organizational structure of the nation-state and its dominant political culture that invariably impacts regional and local identity, marginalizing them, denying them what they perceive as their legitimate claim over national resources and not granting them their rightful place in the socio-political and economic fabric of the nation. However, they do not wish to operate outside the national political system. Thus, regionalist and communitarian discourses are often shaped by aspirations and ambitions of the regional middle class who aim to carve out a distinct niche of their own in national life.

Such a politics of difference is often fraught with internal tensions. As leaders and representatives of diverse social groups and cultural regions, they contest the power of the dominant national elite. However, in their own social context, they tend to uphold their superior class positions. As middle-class individuals, they also partake in the consumption culture with as much excitement and enthusiasm as anyone else. While they ask for accommodation in the emergent national power structure, they do not seem to be opposed to their positions of privilege in their own local context.

Margins and the Middle Class

Besides the diversities and differences of regional identities, linguistic cultures, and other horizontal communitarian identities, the pre-existing marginalities of caste and tribe are also sources of diversity within the middle classes of India. The social order of caste in India has been based on notions of hierarchy, exclusion, and discrimination/denial (Jodhka 2012). Individual mobility was simply not possible or allowed in the traditional system. This was particularly difficult for those located lower down in the caste hierarchy, the untouchables or the Dalits.

After independence from colonial rule, the democratic Indian state institutionalized a system of affirmative action. Following the initiatives taken up by the colonial state during the first half of the 20th century, the Indian state identified the most deprived communities and listed them as Scheduled Castes (SCs). Similarly, the social groups living in relative isolation were classified as Scheduled Tribes (STs). The state introduced a special quota for the two categories under which seats, approximating to their proportions in the total population, were reserved for them in educational institutions, government jobs, and legislative bodies up to the highest level—the Indian Parliament. The Indian government also introduced several other legislative and developmental measures targeted specifically for the benefit of such groups and communities.

In addition to these provisions, constitutionally applicable at the national level, some states of the Indian union have had their own quota regimes, which reserve jobs and seats in educational institutions at the state level for the other 'backward' castes and communities, identified locally. Following recommendations of various commissions set up by the Government of India to identify 'classes' that remain 'backward', other than those listed as SCs, the union government also decided to reserve jobs and seats in state-funded educational institutions for the Other Backward Classes (OBCs).

Though confined to a small proportion of the total population of the scheduled communities, the quotas did begin a process of individual social mobility among historically deprived social groups and categories, the SCs and STs. Over the years a new middle-class elite has emerged from amongst these communities. Even when the social groups they come from largely remain poor and marginalized, individuals from these communities have been able to move up to senior positions in political institutions, bureaucracy, and academia.

In normal course, an upwardly mobile individual gradually moves out of his/her group of origin to another group compatible with his/her class location. This, however, has generally not been the experience of mobility among those from the untouchable castes of the Indian social order. Even when they move to secular employment and middle-class occupation, their identification with the communities of their origin tends to remain strong. Why does this happen?

First and foremost, economic mobility does not always lead to a disappearance of the prejudice of the dominant groups. Consequently, social mobility that should accompany the individual's economic mobility is limited. Even when they occupy high positions of authority, their colleagues identify them through their communities of origin and they find it hard to socially integrate themselves in the work place (see Jodhka 2015; Prakash 2015). The experience of individual mobility in society, where caste identities embedded with notions of hierarchy and prejudice remain strong, produces a sense of anger and agitation among them. They turn back to their communities with the realization that without a larger social change which gives dignity to their communities, their individual achievements are of limited value.

Upwardly mobile SCs also find it difficult to realize their middle-class status because of their immediate family contexts. Given that such an individual is likely to be the first or second generation person with a middle-class salary, s/he is unlikely to have other resources, such as an urban house or social networks, that enable the stabilizing of such a process of mobility. Such mobile Dalits are often among the first members of their kinship to move to an economically secure position; they are invariably expected to 'help' other members of the family. The most obvious mode of doing this is through sending a portion of their income home to poor parents and other family members (Naudet 2014: 244). They also help members of their extended kin in their efforts of economic and social mobility and they often do so with a sense of commitment (Srinivas 2008; Prakash 2015), as a source of overcoming their distance from the communities of their origin (Jodhka 2015: 169–210). Such a role also implies sharing their incomes with the larger community and compromising on one's own aspirations.

Perhaps the most important reason for the primacy of community identity over class identity among the upwardly mobile Dalits is the moral imperative of 'paying back' (Naudet 2008, 2014; Ciotti 2010). Even though mobility through education, followed by a job, is an individual achievement, the community tends to see educated members of their caste groups as a 'collectively shared' resource (Ciotti 2010). This moral imperative also works on individuals. Given that an SC individual invariably acquires education and a secure job using quotas, which are viewed as an outcome of the larger community's struggle for their rights, s/he finds it hard to be indifferent to the communitarian context of his/her mobility.

Speaking to upwardly mobile Dalits, Jules Naudet repeatedly found his respondents insisting on 'the need to maintain strong bonds with the group of origin'. He writes:

> These people's successes are cases of an individual's success. It is a person, at most, a family, who benefits from this mobility. And yet, these individuals choose to speak of their mobility as if it were the community as a whole that was elevated by their success. Even though some of them acknowledge the individual character of their success, they still place their individual story within the wider frame of their groups. (Naudet 2014: 245)

However, notwithstanding this sense of identification with the social group of their origin and the politics of caste discrimination, their mobility out of the community also inhibits their return. While they realize the need for change through political mobilization and activism, they are no longer similar to those they have left behind and feel a sense of alienation from their communities (Guru 2001). They tend to form their own enclaves where they feel comfortable by expanding the boundaries of their caste communities through categories such as the Dalits. This also gives them the sense of a new identity, a sense of being modern and dignified. Thus, they form a new community with individuals from similar social backgrounds and political orientations. Their social interactions are also likely to be limited to fellow Dalits (Ram 1988). Guru puts this very sharply in the following words:

> The dalit middle class members are psychologically excluded from the larger middle class imagination.... Upper caste middle class show unprecedented intolerance towards dalit officers.... [They] take extraordinary care to see that dalits are not able to buy houses in their locality.... The dalits find themselves shunted out to the outskirts of the cities.... (Guru 2001: 145–6)

This middle class on the margins also tends to think differently. Their perception of the state and economy is often shaped by the prism of caste and the associated hierarchies and discrimination experienced by members of their community, if not by themselves. Hence, their image and understanding of India's modernity is generally at variance with that of the dominant section of the middle class. A good example of this is their attitude towards economic liberalization. Even though they carry a sense of pride for being middle class because they perceive their status as being an acquired virtue of merit rather than an ascribed attribute of caste origin (Guru 2001: 144), they do not undermine the critical role of the state policy of quotas in their own personal mobility. They still look up to the state which alone, for many of them, could be above caste-ridden institutions of the civil society and market economy. Recognition of the deficits of social and cultural capital in their communities also makes them suspect advocates of free market and meritorious regimes. Even when they mobilize for their increased participation in the neo-liberal market economy, they seek quotas and state support.

Similarly, the Adivasi middle class invokes the politics of diversity to preserve their rights over natural resources. They tend to join their communities in opposing large-scale developmental projects in tribal concentrated pockets. Given that they are mostly concentrated in mineral rich parts of the country; such projects often end up alienating tribal communities from the resources they always had access to. However, the Adivasi middle class is often not able to put up a common front in support of their demand due to their vast internal diversity in terms of language, religion, and spatial presence. Substantial sections of the middle class amongst Adivasis, particularly in the North Eastern part of India, are also part of various ethnic movements seeking recognition and political autonomy from the Indian state.

Beyond the diversities of region, religion, language, caste, and tribe, the Indian middle class also has diversities of orientation and ideology. A large number of individuals from the mainstream middle class actively dissociate themselves from its normative life style and actively participate in a variety of social movements and work with civil society organizations in far-flung areas of the country. They articulate a variety of alternative ways of organizing social, economic, and political relationships. Radical left-wing formations and movements of marginalized groups against big dams and corporate take-over of common resources have invariably been led by urban educated members of the middle classes.

Conclusion

India is known to be a land of tradition, often represented through its village life, caste hierarchy, and religious communities. While this image persists, the ground has shifted. Even though demographically nearly two-thirds of the Indian population continues to live in its rural settlements and caste and religious sentiments have not gone away, yet over the past century and more, a modern middle class has also grown in the country. More importantly perhaps, the category of 'middle class' is increasingly becoming a preferred source of self-identification, particularly among the rapidly growing numbers of mobile Indians.

As is widely known, the modern middle class in India was an offshoot of the British colonial rule, born during the Macaulay moment, when they needed a class of clerks who had a working knowledge of the English language and could be employed in their service for carrying out the administrative tasks of the expanding empire. The introduction of English education also enabled a section of the erstwhile local elite to educate their children in the Western system of learning and join the ranks of professionals, lawyers, doctors, and teachers, in the empire. Over the years, its size and spread increased; so did its aspirations. Members of the middle class actively participated in the freedom movement and were at the forefront of articulating the idea of India as a modern nation-state.

Among those who initiated the articulation of a middle-class identity for Indians was the first prime minister of the country, Pandit Jawaharlal Nehru. 'I am, of course, a middle-class person', he is reported to have claimed (Baviskar and Ray 2011: 5). Being a middle-class person in the India of the 1950s and 1960s meant many things. It meant inhabiting 'a particular orientation towards modernity', a mindset that was different from that of an industrial worker, a peasant, or a landlord. It also meant being open-minded and egalitarian; following the rule of law and not being swayed by private motives or particularistic agenda;

being fiscally prudent and living within one's means; embracing science and rationality in the public sphere; setting aside the primordial loyalties of caste and kinship; opening oneself to new affinities and associations based on merit, and to identities forged in the workplace (Baviskar and Ray 2011: 5–6).

These universalistic claims had political effects. They enabled the middle class to acquire a position of power and authority, as agents of building a modern nation. The middle class took upon itself the task of defining goals and priorities for the newly liberated country. While communities, cultivators, workers, industrialists, or armed forces all constituted the new nation, it was the middle class that was to become the fountainhead of modern India. It carried on its shoulders the responsibility of being representative of all categories of Indians (Varma 1998; Deshpande 2003; Fernandes 2011; Baviskar and Ray 2011).

No one gained as much from India's independence from colonial rule as the Indian middle class. Not only were a substantial proportion of the leadership that inherited power from the colonial rulers middle-class professionals, the process of nation building and economic development also put them at the centre stage of the emerging nation-state. They were at the helm of public and political affairs. Their self-acquired responsibility of setting the agenda for the country gave the middle class immense power and enabled its manifold expansion.

Development was equated with modernization, liberal democracy, economic growth, and secularism. The middle class was both the cause and the consequence of these processes. They articulated the need for a self-reliant India, a political requirement and an imperative of Independence. These initiatives also helped the new state acquire legitimacy to intervene in social, cultural, and economic spheres with its policies and programmes of developing India. The state promoted industrialization, a variety of modern institutions, and a mammoth developmental bureaucracy. These initiatives were supposed to help the new nation in achieving self-reliance, ameliorate poverty, and enhance the capabilities of its citizens by providing health and education.

However, by the late 1980s, the processes of economic development and democratization began to produce their own contradictions. While on one hand, demands of the rapidly changing global economic environment and growing pressure from the private capital within the country made it necessary for India to pursue a policy of liberalization and loosening of state controls, on the other hand 'new' voices for the expansion of democratic rights began to emerge from the margins of Indian society. These had far-reaching implications for the Indian middle class.

The process of economic liberalization initiated by India during the early 1990s completely changed the script of the Indian middle-class story. Given that it had already consolidated its social and economic position in the national economy, it found it rather easy to switch over to the promising private sector. The shift in economic policy and the changed global environment enabled Indian economy to grow at a much faster pace. The middle class grew along with it. The engine of growth this time was private capital. This growth required educated and technically skilled personnel, which expanded the ranks of the middle class.

The process of economic growth, some argue, is fundamentally changing the social structure of India, from a society characterized by 'a sharp contrast between a small elite and a large impoverished mass, to being one with substantial intermediate classes' (Sridharan 2008: 27). Unlike the 'old' middle class, this new Indian middle class was not only located outside the state-system, but it also no longer carried the burden of nation building. The nation had already been built and the middle class saw itself as its evidence. Its mandate this time was to live for itself, through endless consumption. Consumption, for the neo-liberal middle class, was not simply an act of self-indulgence but also a source of identity.

The neo-liberal middle class advocates a different set of values that go well with the new economic regime of efficiency, merit, and competition. Policies of affirmative action begin to be seen as breeding inefficiency, nepotism, and mediocrity. The state, they argue, should focus its energy on building infrastructure, which would further galvanize the markets and help in economic growth. The Indian state had already done the job of laying its foundations and it need no longer be directly active beyond its basic function of providing good governance, financial management, and security.

As popularly understood, the market-centric economic system requires creation of an environment where consumption exceeds production, which in turn ensures realization of profits. Further, for its growth, such an economic system needs an efficient and skilled workforce. The expansion of the middle class is the answer to both. An expanding middle class also becomes a natural source of producing legitimacy for a market-centric economy. It becomes a norm for the larger society, a space where everyone (except the rich!) wants to be, it also becomes a medium of defining what is good for society. Its access to media makes it easier for it to accomplish this task.

However, expansion also brings diversity. While the values that the middle class advocates acquire a kind of hegemony, they do not go uncontested from those who stand at its margins. The Indian middle class remains a story full of complexities without a simple or linear trajectory: socially, culturally, and politically. The sociology of the Indian middle class is even more complex than its history. As we have discussed in different chapters, though pioneers of the Indian middle-class story spoke in a universalistic language, they also promoted particularistic identities, primarily to preserve their privileges of caste, class, and gender. By implication, such moves kept them divided on regional, religious, and linguistic lines.

The middle-class story is also not merely a linear trajectory of upper caste or patriarchal domination.

As an ideological process, the evolving state system in India could be different from the everyday practices of its agents. This is reflected in the constitutional commitments of the new regime, which require it to initiate policies and programmes towards ensuring the creation of enablers for equal opportunity. Over the years, the programmes of social engineering from above and growing democratic assertion from below have successfully carved out spaces for marginalized social groups within the larger domain of the nation and the middle class. Thanks to the policies of affirmative action, a small but important section of the middle class evolved from within the marginalized social groups over a period of time.

These processes also make the political arena a contested space. The newly emergent elite from the margins tend to pursue a politics of social justice. They demand for expansion of affirmative action programmes, a more active and interventionist state that would create an enabling environment for them to enter the skewed fields of the market economy and help in upward economic mobility of the members of their communities. They also find support for their position from sections of mainstream civil society organizations, social movements, and a variety of individuals.

However, the dominant sections of traditionally privileged groups, the upper castes, actively contest such formulations.

The normative hegemony of the middle class acquires significance because it begins to shape mobility patterns and value parameters. A good example of this is what has come to be described as the aspirational middle class. The idea of the *aspirational middle class* has also come to shape the political discourse in Indian democracy. The Election Manifesto of a major national party describes them as those 'who have risen from the category of poor and are yet to stabilize in the middle class', the 'neo middle class'.[1]

These 'upwardly mobile poor' are invariably young men and women who have acquired modern education through one of the hundreds of thousands of colleges spread across the country giving degree/

[1] Election manifesto of the Bharatiya Janata Party for the 2014 General Elections, available at http://www.bjp.org/images/pdf_2014/full_manifesto_english_07.04.2014.pdf (accessed on 7 March 2015).

diploma courses in information and technology, marketing, law, finance, business, or tourism. Many of them have moved from rural areas to urban locations by selling their parental assets and have entered into the field of transport, manage small businesses, work as sales executives in big consumer retails or as supervisors in showrooms of big corporates, offer utility maintenance services, and perform the role of delivery agents or clerks with an e-commerce company. Countless numbers of them are employed in the new business economy of supplying goods and services to middle- and upper-middle-class homes.

Quite like the consumption-driven middle class, this category of workers has also largely grown during the post-liberalization period. They have grown along with the expanding urban economy. They aspire for a place in the Indian growth story and hope to eventually climb up within the private economy. However, their realities remain precarious. Many of them are first generation young migrants from villages or small towns and relatively less developed pockets of the country. Significant proportions of them remain employed in the informal sector or in an informal/insecure mode. They stay in pooled accommodations, often shared between five and six people. They eat their food at small roadside eateries and buy clothes and products that are imitations of established brands. Some, who are middle aged, live in cramped apartments having left their families in their native hinterland and lead lives of forced bachelorhood. Those who live with their families do so by living in irregular/unauthorized urban settlements or in lower income group quarters in the urban peripheries. The rents they pay for their accommodation far exceeds what they can afford. They travel long distances for work. Their living conditions further deteriorate with the gradual and steady withdrawal of the state and entry of private players for providing water, electricity, transport, and other basic amenities. The most prized possession of the better-off in this class is invariably a two-wheeler, a 'smart' cell phone, and, occasionally, a laptop. For the young in this category, the internet, films, and occasional strolls in the malls are the only sources of leisure.

Pinned down between the self-image and aspiration of being middle class on one hand and the social and economic realities that accompany low-income groups in urban centres on the other, they almost always live in a state of anxiety, struggling between the needs of supporting their families, paying educational fees of second- or third-grade private English medium schools of their children, and maintaining the appearance of not being poor. This creates a self-constructed space where they sway between conformity and bitterness with regards to the larger social and economic systems, the political arrangements, and choices they make for themselves and their families. Quite like their personal lives, their politics is also unpredictable. While this neo-middle class is indeed an unstable social, economic, and political formation, its presence is functional for the hegemonic project of the Indian middle class, particularly in the context of widespread inequalities and its size being relatively small in proportional terms.

However, its presence could also be a challenge, potentially destabilizing. Thus the hegemonic project of middle class remains fragile, and is often contested, both from within and without. As we have repeatedly argued, even when it insists on the need for universalistic norms that value individual merit, it has never shed its own ascriptive identities. These identities often turn into cleavages and conflicts in times of scarcities and inter-individual competition.

Sections within the middle class also become a source of conflict. For example, the upper segments of the middle class, who also tend to be from traditionally privileged or upper caste backgrounds, oppose state-initiated redistributive measures, subsidies, and expenditure on basic well-being. They perceive them as wastage of resources. This is also because of their personal trajectories. They no longer depend on state services as many of them have simply withdrawn into private residential enclaves, away from the hustle, bustle, and dirt of city life. They seem to prefer the provision of the hitherto public goods like water, sanitation, transport or schooling of their children from private providers. In contrast, withdrawal of the state from such service provisions severely hurts the lower sections of the middle class and the aspirational neo-middle class who expect security and subsidy from the state and view privatization of public services negatively.

Different sections of the middle class also have divergent perspectives on the question of representation. While the upper segment of the middle class prefers technocratic and professional solutions to the questions of governance, those on the margins seek proportional representation. Along with those below them, the lower segments of the middle classes often articulate their concerns through the language of rights and view market-based solutions with suspicion. Thus, notwithstanding its hegemonic claims, the Indian middle class remains a contested space.

The politics of India in the coming decades is going to be increasingly shaped by these contestations. The future of India will lie in the ability of the political regimes to channelize these contestations into institutionalized democratic processes such that political articulations/contestations and representations translate into growth and equitable (re)distribution.

References

Ablett, Jonathan, Adarsh Baijal, Eric Beinhocker, Anupam Bose, Diana Farrell, Ulrich Gersch, Ezra Greenberg, Shishir Gupta, and Sumit Gupta. 2007. 'The "Bird of Gold": The Rise of India's Consumer Market', Mckinsey Global Institute, San Francisco. Available at http://www.mckinsey.com/global-themes/asia-pacific/the-bird-of-gold (accessed on 26 January 2016).

Alavi, Hamza. 1975. 'Roots of Underdevelopment: India and the Colonial Mode of Production'. *Economic and Political Weekly* 10(33–5): 1235–62.

Alivelu, G. 2010. 'Salient Aspects of the Growth Story of Indian Railways 1981–82 Through 2007–08'. Working Paper No. 86, Centre for Economic and Social Studies, Begumpet, Hyderabad.

Appadurai, Arjun and Carol A. Breckenridge. 2005. 'Public Modernity in India'. In Carol A. Breckenridge (ed.), *Consuming Modernity: Public Culture in South Asian World*, 1–22. Minneapolis: University of Minnesota Press.

Asian Development Bank. 2010. *The Rise of Asia's Middle Class*. Manila: Asian Development Bank.

Austin, Granville. 1966. *The Indian Constitution: Cornerstone of a Nation*. Oxford: Clarendon Press.

Balakrishnan, Pulapre. 2007. 'The Recovery of India: Economic Growth in the Nehru Era'. *Economic and Political Weekly* 42(45/46): 52–66.

Banerjee, Abhijit and Esther Duflo. 2008. 'What Is Middle Class about the Middle Classes around the World?' *Journal of Economic Perspectives* 22(2): 3–28.

Bardhan, Pranab. 1984. *The Political Economy of Development in India*. New Delhi: Oxford University Press.

Baviskar, Amita. 2011. 'Cows, Cars and Cycle Rickshaws: Bourgeois Environmentalism and Battle for Delhi Streets'. In Amita Baviskar and Raka Ray (eds), *Elite and Everyman: The Cultural Politics of the Indian Middle Classes*, 1–23. New Delhi: Routledge.

Bayly, Alan Christopher. 2012. *Development and Sentiment: Sarvepalli Gopal and the Political Thought of Nehru's India*. First Dr. S. Gopal Annual Memorial Lecture, delivered at King's College London.

Beinhocker, Eric D., Dianna Farrell, and Adil S. Zainulbhai. 2007. 'Tracking the Growth of India's Middle Class'. *The McKinsey Quarterly*, no. 3.

Beteille, Andre. 2001. 'The Indian Middle-class'. *The Hindu*, 5 February.

————. 2013. 'Does Middle Class Have Boundaries'. In Surinder S. Jodhka (ed.), *Interrogating India's Modernity: Democracy, Identity and Citizenship*. New Delhi: Oxford University Press.

Bhatia, B.M. 1994. *India's Middle Class: Role in Nation Building*. New Delhi: Konark Publishers.

Bourdieu, Pierre. 1984. *Distinction: A Social Critique of the Judgment of Taste*. Trans. Richard Nice. Cambridge, MA: Harvard University Press.

————. 1990. *The Logic of Practice*. Trans. Richard Nice. Stanford: Stanford University Press.

Brosius, Christiane. 2010. *India's Middle Class: New Forms of Urban Leisure, Consumption and Prosperity*. New Delhi: Routledge.

Byres, Terence J. 1997. 'State, Class and Development Planning in India'. In Terence J. Byres (ed.), *The State, Development Planning and Liberalisation in India*, 36–81. New Delhi: Oxford University Press.

Chatterjee, Partha. 1990. 'The Nationalist Resolution of the Women's Question'. In Kumkum Sangari and Sudesh Vaid (eds), *Recasting Women: Essays in Indian Colonial History*. New Brunswick: Rutgers University Press.

————. 1993. *The Nation and Its Fragment*. New Jersey: Princeton University Press.

————. 1997. 'Development Planning and the Indian State'. In Terence J. Byres (ed.), *The State, Development*

Planning and Liberalisation in India, 82–104. New Delhi: Oxford University Press.

————. 2011. 'Against Corruption = Against Politics'. Available at http://kafila.org/2011/08/28/against-corruption-against-politics-partha-chatterjee/ (accessed on 16 February 2015).

Chaudhuri, Maitrayee. 1993. *The Indian Women's Movement: Reform and Revival*. Delhi: Radiant (Reprinted 2010, Delhi: Palm Leaf Publications).

————. 1995. 'Citizens, Workers and Emblems of Culture: An Analysis of the First Plan Document on Women'. *Contributions to Indian Sociology* 29 (1 and 2): 211–35.

————. 2014. 'Gender, Media and Popular Culture in a Global India'. In Leela Fernandes (ed.), *Routledge Handbook of Gender in South Asia*. London: Routledge.

Chibber, Vivek. 2003. *Locked in Place: State Building and Late Industrialisation in India*. New Jersey: Princeton University Press.

Ciotti, Manuela. 2010. *Retro-modern India: Forging the Low Caste Self*. New Delhi: Routledge.

Cole, G. D. H. 1950. 'The Conception of the Middle-classes'. *The British Journal of Sociology* 1(4): 275–90.

Dahrendorf, Ralph. 1959. *Class and Class Conflict in Industrial Society*. Stanford: Stanford University Press.

Desai, Sonalde. 2001. 'A Tale of Two Middle Classes'. Mimeo, National Council of Applied Economic Research.

Available at http://www.sonaldedesai.org/a-tale-of-two-middle-classe.pdf (accessed on 15 February 2015).

Deshpande, Satish. 2003. *Contemporary India: A Sociological View*. New Delhi: Penguin Books.

Dickey, Sara. 2012. 'The Pleasures and Anxieties of Being in the Middle: Emerging Middle-Class Identities in Urban South India'. *Modern Asian Studies* 46(3): 559–99.

Dyck, Steffen et al. 2009. 'Asia's Rising Middle Class: A Force to be Reckoned With'. Deutsche Bank Research. Available at http://www.esocialsciences.org/Download/repecDownl ... &AId=2232&fref=repec (accessed on 15 February 2015).

Earle, Peter. 1989. *The Making of the English Middle Class: Business, Society and Family Life in London 1660–1730*. Berkeley and Los Angeles: University of California Press.

Easterly, William. 2001. 'The Middle Class Consensus on Economic Development'. Mimeo, The World Bank, Washington. Available at https://williameasterly.files.wordpress.com/2010/08/34_easterly_middleclassconsensus_prp.pdf (accessed on 15 February 2015).

Ernst and Young. Undated. 'Hitting the Sweet Spot: The Growth of the Middle Class in Emerging Markets'. Available at http://www.ey.com/Publication/vwLUAssets/Hitting_the_sweet_spot/$FILE/Hitting_the_sweet_spot.pdf (accessed on 10 December 2014).

Esping-Andersen, Gosta. 1990. *The Three Worlds of Welfare Capitalism*. Cambridge: Polity Press.

Fernandes, Leela. 2000. 'Restructuring the New Middle Class in Liberalizing India'. *Comparative Studies of South Asia, Africa and Middle East* 20(1 and 2): 88–104.

——. 2006. *India's New Middle-class: Democratic Politics in an era of Economic Reform*. Minneapolis: University of Minnesota Press.

——. 2011. 'Hegemony and Inequality: Theoretical Reflections on India's "New" Middle Class'. In Amita Baviskar and Raka Ray (eds), *Elite and Everyman: The Cultural Politics of the Indian Middle Classes*, 58–82. New Delhi: Routledge.

Fernandes, Leela and Patrick Heller. 2006. 'Hegemonic Aspirations: New Middle Class Politics and India's Democracy in Comparative Perspective'. *Critical Asian Studies* 38(4): 495–522.

Frankel, Francine. 1978. *India's Political Economy*. New Jersey: Princeton University Press.

Frankel, Francine and M.S.A. Rao. 1989. *Dominance and State Power in Modern India: Decline of a Social Order*. New Delhi: Oxford University Press.

French, Wilham E. 1996. *A Peaceful and Working People: Manners, Morals and Class Formation in Northern Mexico*. New Mexico: Albuquerque University.

Fuller, C.J. and Haripriya Narasimhan. 2007. 'Information Technology Professionals and the New-Rich Middle Class in Chennai (Madras)'. *Modern Asian Studies* 41(1): 121–50.

Ganguly-Scrase, Ruchika. 2003. 'Paradoxes of Globalization: Liberalization, and Gender Equality: The Worldviews of the Lower Middle Class in West Bengal, India'. *Gender & Society* 17(4): 544–66.

Gemici, Kurtulus. 2007. 'Karl Polanyi and the Antinomies of Embeddedness'. *Socio-Economic Review* 6(1): 1–29.

Giddens, Anthony. 1981. *The Class Structure of the Advanced Societies.* London: Hutchinson.

Goldthrope, John. 1963. *The Affluent Worker: Political Attitudes and Behaviour.* Cambridge: Cambridge University Press.

Gooptu, Nandini. 2001. *The Politics of the Urban Poor in Early Twentieth-Century India.* Cambridge: Cambridge University Press.

Gouldner, Alvin. 1979. *The Future of Intellectuals and the Rise of the New Class.* New York: Seabury Press.

Government of India (GOI). 2009. *The Challenge of Employment: An Informal Sector Perspective, Vol. I*, pp. 10–15. National Commission for Enterprises in Unorganised Sector, New Delhi.

―――. 2012. *Annual Report of Ministry of Personnel, Public Grievance and Pensions.* New Delhi.

Grewal, J.S. 1989. 'Changing Sikh Self-Image before Independence'. In P. C. Chatterjee (ed.), *Self Image Identity and Nationalism.* Shimla: Indian Institute of Advanced Studies.

Gupta, Dipankar. 2000. *Mistaken Modernity: India between Worlds.* New Delhi: HarperCollins Publishers India.

Gupta, Dipankar. 2009. *The Caged Phoenix: Can India Fly?* New Delhi: Penguin Books.

Guru, Gopal. 2001. 'Dalit Middle Class Hangs in Air'. In Imtiaz Ahmad and Helmut Reifeld (eds), *Middle Class Values in India and Western Europe*. New Delhi: Social Science Press.

Harriss, John. 2007. 'Antinomies of Empowerment Observations on Civil Society, Politics and Urban Governance in India'. *Economic and Political Weekly* 42(26): 2716–24.

Harriss-White, Barbara. 2003. *India Working: Essay on Society and Economy*. Cambridge: Cambridge University Press.

ILER. 2013. *Indian Labour and Employment Report*. New Delhi: Academic Foundation.

Imtiaz Ahmad and Helmut Reifeld (eds). 2001. *Middle Class Values in India and Western Europe*. New Delhi: Social Science Press.

Jaffrelot, Christophe and Peter van der Veer. 2008. 'Introduction'. In Christophe Jaffrelot and Peter van der Veer (eds), *Patterns of Middle Class Consumption in India and China*, 11–34. New Delhi: Sage.

Jha, Prem Shankar. 1980. *The Political Economy of Stagnation*. Delhi: Oxford University Press.

Jodhka, Surinder S. (ed.). 2001. *Community and Identities: Contemporary Discourses on Culture and Politics in India*. New Delhi: Sage.

———. 2012. *Caste: Oxford India Short Introductions*. New Delhi: Oxford University Press.

————. 2014. 'Emergent Ruralities: Revisiting Village Life and Agrarian Change in Haryana'. *Economic and Political Weekly* 49(26 and 27): 5–17.

————. 2015. *Caste in Contemporary India*. New Delhi: Routledge.

John, Mary. 1996. 'Gender and Development in India, 1970–1990'. *Economic and Political Weekly* 31(47): 3071–7.

Joshi, P. C. 1979. 'Dimensions of Agricultural Planning: Reflections on the Mahalanobis Approach'. *Man and Development* 4: 9–31.

Joshi, Sanjay. 2001. *Fractured Modernity: Making of Middle Class in Colonial North India*. New Delhi: Oxford University Press.

Kamath, Lalitha and M. Vijayabaskar. 2009. 'Limits and Possibilities of Middle-class Associations as Urban Collective Actors'. *Economic and Political Weekly* 44(26 and 27): 368–76.

Kapur, Devesh. 2010. 'The Middle Class in India: A Social Formation or Political Actor?' *Political Power and Social Theory* 21: 143–69.

Kaur, Ravinder and Surjit Bhalla. 2015. 'No Proof Required: Sons, Daughters, Class'. *Indian Express*, 18 August.

Kaviraj, Sudipta. 2010. 'A State of Contradictions: The Post-colonial State in India'. In Sudipta Kaviraj (ed.), *The Imaginary Institutions of India: Politics and Ideas*, 210–33. Ranikhet: Permanent Black.

Kerschner, Edward and Naeema Huq. 2011. 'Asia's Affluence: The Emerging 21st Century Middle Class'. Morgan

Stanley and Smith and Barney. Available at http://www. morganstanleyfa.com/public/projectfiles/35257b34- b160-45e4-980d-8bca327db92b.pdf (accessed on 15 February 2015).

Khilnani, Sunil. 1997. *The Idea of India*. New Delhi: Penguin Books.

Kidambi, Prashant. 2012. 'Becoming Middle Class: The Local History of a Global Story'. In A. Richard Lopez and Barbara Weinstein (eds), *The Making of a Middle Class: Towards a Transnational History.* Durham, North Carolina: Duke University Press.

Kochhar, Rajesh. 2004. 'Denationalised Middle Class Global Escape from Mandal'. *Economic and Political Weekly* 39(1): 20.

Kohli, Atul. 1987. *State and Poverty in India: The Politics of Reform*. Cambridge: Cambridge University Press in Association with Orient Longman.

——————. March 1989. 'Politics of Economic Liberalization in India'. *World Development*, 305–28.

——————. 2008. 'Politics of Economic Growth in India 1980–2005'. *Economic and Political Weekly* 41(14): 1361–70.

——————. 2011. 'India's Fragmented Multi-Cultural State and Protected Industrialisation'. In Atul Kohli (ed.), *Democracy and Development in India: From Socialism to Pro-Business*, 107–39. New Delhi: Oxford University Press.

Kothari, Rajni. 1970. *Politics in India*. Hyderabad: Orient Longman.

————. 1991. 'State and Statelessness in Our Time'. *Economic and Political Weekly* 26(11/12): 553–5; 557–8.

Krishna, Sankaran. 2006. 'The Bomb, Biography and the Indian Middle-class'. *Economic and Political Weekly* 41(23): 2327–31.

Kundu, Debolina. 2011. 'Elite Capture in Participatory Urban Governance'. *Economic and Political Weekly* 46(10): 23–5.

Lahiri, Ashok. 2014. 'The Middle Class and Economic Reforms'. *Economic and Political Weekly* 49(11): 37–44.

Landry, Bart and Kris Marsh. 2011. 'The Evolution of the New Black Middle Class'. *Annual Review of Sociology* 37: 373–94.

Lefebvre, Bertrand. 2008. 'The Indian Corporate Hospitals: Touching Middle Class Lives'. In Christophe Jaffrelot and Peter van der Veer (eds), *Patterns of Middle Class Consumption in India and China*, 88–109. New Delhi: Sage.

Liechty, Mark. 2003. *Suitably Modern: Making Middle-Class Culture in a New Consumer Society*. Princeton, NJ: Princeton University Press.

Lockwood, D. 1958. *The Blackcoated Worker: A Study in Class Consciousness*. Oxford: Clarendon Press.

Mahalanobis, P.C. 1955. 'The Approach of Operational Research to Planning in India'. *Sankhya: The Indian Journal of Statistics* 1 and 2: 3–62.

Maitra, Sudeshna. 2007. 'Who Are the Indian Middle Class? An EM Approach Using Durables Ownership'.

Mimeo, York University. Available at http://www.cid. harvard.edu/neudc07/docs/neudc07_poster_maitra.pdf (accessed on 15 February 2015).

Mani, Lata. 1987. 'Contentious Traditions: The Debate on SATI in Colonial India'. *Cultural Critique* 7 (Autumn): 119–56.

—————. 1999. *Contentious Traditions: The Debate on Sati in Colonial India*. Delhi: Oxford University Press.

Mankekar, Purnima. 1999. *Screening Culture, Viewing Politics: Ethnography of Television, Womanhood, and Nation in Postcolonial India*. Durham: Duke University Press.

Mantena, Karuna. 2012. 'On Gandhi's Critique of the State: Sources, Contexts, Conjunctures'. *Modern Intellectual History* 9(3): 535–63.

Marshall, T.H. 1950. *Citizenship and Social Class, and Other Essays*. Cambridge: Cambridge University Press.

Mathur, Nita. 2010. 'Shopping Malls, Credit Cards and Global Brands: Consumer Culture and Lifestyle of India's New Middle Class'. *South Asia Research* 30(3): 211–23.

Mazzarella, William. 2004. 'Middle-class'. Available at https://www.soas.ac.uk/south-asia-institute/keywords/file24808.pdf (accessed on 26 January 2016).

Meyer, Christian and Nancy Birdsall. 2012. 'New Estimates of India's Middle Class: Technical Note'. Mimeo, Center for Global Development. Available at http://www. cgdev.org/doc/2013_MiddleClassIndia_TechnicalNote_CGDNote.pdf (accessed on 26 January 2016).

Mishra, B.B. 1961. *The Indian Middle-class.* Delhi: Oxford University Press.

Naudet, Jules. 2008. 'Paying Back to Society: Upward Social Mobility among Dalits'. *Contributions to Indian Sociology* 42(3): 413–14.

———. 2014. 'Finding One's Place among the Elite: How Dalits Experiencing Sharp Upward Social Mobility Adjust to Their New Social Status'. In Clarinda Still (ed.), *Dalits in Neoliberal India.* New Delhi: Routledge.

Nehru, Jawaharlal. 1941. *Towards Freedom: The Autobiography of Jawaharlal Nehru.* New York: The John Day Company.

Owensby, Brian P. 1999. *Intimate Ironies: Modernity and the Making of Middle-Class Lives in Brazil.* Stanford: Stanford University Press.

Oza, Rual. 2006. *The Making of Neoliberal India: Nationalism, Gender, and the Paradoxes of Globalization.* London: Routledge.

Pandian, M.S.S. 2007. *Brahmin and Non-Brahmin: Genealogies of the Tamil Political Present.* Ranikhet: Permanent Black.

Peace, Adrian. 1984. 'Constructions of Class, Images of Inequality: The Middle Class and the Urban Poor in a North Indian City'. *Urban Anthropology* 13(2/3): 261–94.

Polanyi, Karl. 1957. *The Great Transformation: The Political and Economic Origins of Our Times.* Boston: Beacon Press.

Poulantzas, N. 1975. *Classes in Contemporary Capitalism.* London: New Left.

Prakash, Aseem. 2015. *Dalit Capital: State, Markets and Civil Society in Urban India.* New Delhi: Routledge.

Radhakrishnan, Smitha. 2008. 'Examining the "Global" Indian Middle Class: Gender and Culture in the Silicon Valley/Bangalore Circuit'. *Journal of Intercultural Studies* 29(1): 7–20.

Ram, Nandu. 1988. *The Mobile Scheduled Castes: Rise of a New Middle Class.* New Delhi: Hindustan Publishing Corporation.

Rao, V. K. R.V. 1982. *Indian Socialism: Retrospect and Prospect.* New Delhi: Concept Publication.

Ravallion, Martin. 2009. 'The Developing World's Bulging (but Vulnerable) Middle Class'. Policy Research Working Paper 4816. Washington: The World Bank.

Reserve Bank of India (RBI). 2013. *Handbook of Statistics on the Indian Economy 2012–13.* Mumbai.

Roy, Anupama. 2014. 'Gender and Citizenship in India'. In Leela Fernandes (ed.), *Routledge Handbook of Gender in South Asia*, 55–69. London: Routledge.

Rudolph, Lloyd and Susanne Rudolph. 1987. *In Pursuit of Lakshmi: The Political Economy of Indian State.* Chicago: University of Chicago Press.

Rudra, Ashok. 1989. 'Emergence of the Intelligentsia as a Ruling Class in India'. *Economic and Political Weekly* 24(3): 142–50.

Rutten, M.A.F. 1995. *Farms and Factories: Social Profile of Large Farmers and Rural Industrialists in West India.* New Delhi: Oxford University Press.

Sarkar, Sumit. 1983. *Modern India 1885–1947.* New Delhi: Macmillan.

Saxena, Rachna. 2010. 'The Middle Class in India: Issues and Opportunities'. Deutsche Bank Research. Available at http://www.dbresearch.de/PROD/DBR_INTERNET_DE-PROD/PROD0000000000253735.pdf (accessed on 15 February 2015).

Shukla, Rajesh and Roopa Purushothaman. 2008. *Market Information Survey*. National Council for Applied Economic Research, New Delhi.

Sridharan, E. 2008. 'The Political Economy of the Middle Classes in Liberalising India'. ISAS Working Paper No. 49. Available at http://goo.gl/STB9CO (accessed on 26 January 2016).

Srinivas, Gurram. 2008. 'Education and Social Mobility among the Middle Class Dalits'. In L. C. Mallaiah and K.B. Ratna Kumari (eds), *Dalits and Human Development: Contemporary Issues and Emerging Patterns*. Delhi: Abhijeet Publications.

Srivastava, Sanjay. 2009. 'Urban Spaces, and Moral Middle Classes in Delhi'. *Economic and Political Weekly* 44(26–7): 338–45.

————. 2014. Sudden Selves: 'MTI ("Mother Tongue Influence") and Personality Development: The Making of New Labour in North India'. Unpublished seminar paper.

Thakurdas, Purshotamdas, J.R.D. Tata, G.D. Birla, Sir Ardeshir Dalal, Shri Ram Kasturbhai Lalbhai, A.D. Shroff and John Matthai. 1944. *A Plan of Economic Development for India*. New York: Penguin Books.

Thorner, Daniel. 1969. 'Capitalist Farming in India'. *Economic and Political Weekly* 4(52): A211–A212.

Upadhya, Carol. 1988. 'The Farmer-Capitalists of Coastal Andhra Pradesh'. *Economic and Political Weekly* 23(27–8): 1376–82.

—————. 2008. 'Rewriting the Code: Software Professionals and the Reconstitution of Indian Middle Class Identity'. In Christophe Jaffrelot and Peter van der Veer (eds), *Patterns of Middle Class Consumption in India and China*, 55–87. New Delhi: Sage.

Urfi, A. J. 2012. 'Birdwatchers, Middle Class and the "Bharat-India" Divide: Perspectives from Recent Bird Writings'. *Economic and Political Weekly* 47(42): 27–29.

Vanaik, Achin. 1990. *The Painful Transition: Bourgeoisie Democracy in India*. London: Verso.

Varma, Pavan K. 1998. *The Great Indian Middle-class*. New Delhi: Penguin.

Varshney, Ashutosh. 2000. 'Is India Becoming More Democratic?'. *The Journal of Asian Studies* 59(1): 3–25.

Visvesvaraya, M. 1936. *Planned Economy for India*. Bangalore: Bangalore Press.

Voyce, Malcolm. 2007. 'Shopping Malls in India New Social Dividing Practices'. *Economic and Political Weekly* 42(22): 2005–62.

Vyasulu, Vinod. 1989. 'Nehru and the Visvesvaraya Legacy'. *Economic and Political Weekly* 24(30): 1700–4.

Wahrman, Dror. 1995. *Imagining the Middle Class: The Political Representation of Class in Britain, C. 1780–1840*. Cambridge: Cambridge University Press.

Weber, Max. 1946. *From Max Weber: Essays in Sociology*. Introduced, edited, and translated by H.H. Gerth and C. Wright Mills. Oxford: Oxford University Press.

Wright, Eric Olin. 1978. *Class, Crisis and the State*. London: Verso.

Yadav, Yogendra. 2000. 'Understanding the Second Democratic Upsurge: Trends of Bahujan Participation in Electoral Politics in the 1990s'. In Zoya Hasan, Francine Frankel, Rajeev Bhargava, and Balveer Arora (eds), *Transforming India: Social and Political Dynamics of Democracy*, 120–45. Delhi: Oxford University Press.

Zérah, Marie-Hélène. 2007. 'Middle Class Neighbourhood Associations as Political Players in Mumbai'. *Economic and Political Weekly* 42(47): 61–8.

Index